DIVERSITY IN BLACK GREEK-LETTER ORGANIZATIONS

Starting in the early twentieth century and still thriving in the contemporary era, Black Greek-letter organizations (BGLOs) provide support, opportunities, and service for the Black community. Although BGLOs have always been majority-Black organizations, there are small numbers of non-Black individuals who choose to pledge membership. *Diversity in Black Greek-Letter Organizations: Breaking the Line* explores the experiences of these non-Black members who have immersed themselves in organizations rich with Black history and culture. Through in-depth interviews with 34 such members, Wendy Marie Laybourn and Devon R. Goss reveal how and why these individuals come to identify with organizations designed for the uplift of races other than their own. For non-Black BGLO members, the association with a Black organization provides them the opportunity to consider their own racial identities. Although many non-Black BGLO members recount challenges to their membership, the participants in *Diversity in Black Greek-Letter Organizations* ultimately find a sense of belonging with their Black brothers and sisters, which Laybourn and Goss argue can provide an example of the challenges and promises of cross-racial interactions as a whole.

Wendy M. Laybourn is a doctoral candidate in Sociology at the University of Maryland. Her research focuses on the relationship between racial ideology, especially as evidenced through popular culture and raced institutions, and racial and ethnic identity. Wendy's work has appeared in *Ethnic and Racial Studies, Sociology of Race and Ethnicity, Sociology Compass*, and the *Asian Pacific American Law Journal*.

Devon R. Goss is a doctoral candidate in Sociology at the University of Connecticut. Her research examines the color-line, particularly in relation to instances of boundary crossing in typically racialized institutions. Devon's work has appeared in *Sociology Compass*, the *Sociology of Race and Ethnicity*, and *Symbolic Interaction*.

In this remarkable study, the authors examine what non-Black BGLO members can tell us about race, symbolic boundaries, cultural investments, systems of racial stratification, and allyship. This book is an accessible, nuanced, and important piece of scholarship.

Robin R. Means Coleman *is Professor of Communication and Afroamerican and African Studies at the University of Michigan*

How is the difference within Greek-letter organizations navigated? In their book, two up-and-coming sociologists – Wendy Laybourn and Devon Goss – answer this pressing question with aplomb and perspicacity. Their work promises to take the study of collegiate fraternities and sororities, and Black Greek-letter organizations especially, to new heights.

Gregory S. Parks, J.D., Ph.D. *is Associate Dean and Professor, Wake Forest University School of Law*

DIVERSITY IN BLACK GREEK-LETTER ORGANIZATIONS

Breaking the Line

Wendy M. Laybourn and Devon R. Goss

Routledge
Taylor & Francis Group

NEW YORK AND LONDON

First published 2018
by Routledge
711 Third Avenue, New York, NY 10017

and by Routledge
2 Park Square, Milton Park, Abingdon, Oxon OX14 4RN

Routledge is an imprint of the Taylor & Francis Group, an informa business

Library of Congress Cataloging in Publication Data
A catalog record for this book has been requested

ISBN: 978-1-138-62962-2 (hbk)
ISBN: 978-1-138-62963-9 (pbk)
ISBN: 978-1-315-21035-3 (ebk)

Typeset in Bembo
by Taylor & Francis Books

CONTENTS

TABLES

ACKNOWLEDGEMENTS

This book is the result of a community of support. Our mentors Matthew W. Hughey and Rashawn Ray provided unflagging encouragement and guidance throughout this project.

We are thankful for the intellectual community of the University of Maryland Department of Sociology's Critical Race Initiative, where we benefited from conversations about our ideas and comments on preliminary analyses and earlier drafts. We are especially grateful for Joey Brown, Jocelyn Coates, Jonathan Cox, Asiah Gayfield, and Kevin Winstead. Many other colleagues were generous in their time in reading and commenting on drafts, and we would like to acknowledge Aisha Upton, Stephen Del Visco, and Amy Baugher for their helpful suggestions.

We also wish to thank the folks at Taylor & Francis, especially Amanda Yee and Dean Birkenkamp, for their help and dedication throughout the process. Thank you to France Winddance Twine for her assistance in the early stages of this book project.

Chapter 3 was adapted from a previously published article, and we thank the journal and its editors for their support. An earlier version of the chapter was published as "'You're either one of us or you're not': Racial Hierarchy and Non-Black Members of Black Greek-Letter Organizations," in *Sociology of Race and Ethnicity*. We are grateful for Sage Publications in allowing us to reprint portions of the article.

Finally, this project would not have been possible without the non-Black members of Black Greek-letter organizations who shared their experiences with us.

INTRODUCTION

"Why Would You Do That?": Non-Black Members of Black Fraternities and Sororities

In 1946, *Ebony* magazine featured an article on Bernard Levin, the first white member of Alpha Phi Alpha fraternity (*Ebony Magazine* 1946a). He pledged the Theta Chapter at the University of Illinois at Chicago in June of that year. As one might expect, pledging Levin was not met without controversy. After all, he was joining the first official Black fraternity. Established in 1906 at Cornell University with the intent to ensure the retention of Black college men and serve as a source of support against racial isolation on campus, Alpha Phi Alpha Fraternity, Incorporated ignited a collegiate movement for racial uplift that continued in the Black fraternities and sororities that followed. *Ebony* describes how Alpha brothers approached Levin's admission from two distinct perspectives: there were those who sought to protect the history and tradition of the brotherhood among "the cream of college-bred Negroes"; and those who sought to embrace racial diversity (*Ebony Magazine* 1946b:26). In the end, those advocating for racial diversity prevailed. Levin was pledged, and the first white Alpha member "was embraced as a full fraternity brother" (*Ebony Magazine* 1946b:26).

From accounts of the event, it is unclear the extent of the racial repercussions Levin faced from either side of the color-line. The *Ebony* article simply notes that some of Levin's friends "'viewed with alarm' his initiation into a Negro fraternity" (*Ebony Magazine* 1946b:26). However, eight years later, in 1954, when the University of Kansas' Upsilon Chapter pledged its first white Alpha Phi Alpha member, Roger Lee Youmans, the price of crossing the line was clear. Not only did Youmans's family try to dissuade him from pledging but also after becoming an Alpha, some of his close childhood friends stopped associating with him (Parks 2000). White opposition to his membership spread across his college campus, culminating in a burning cross on his family's front lawn. The cross-burning provided a clear indication of perceptions of Youmans's betrayal of whiteness. A well-known symbol of hate and an image of terror, cross-burning is "a tool for the intimidation and harassment of racial minorities, Catholics, Jews, Communists, and any other groups hated by the Klan" (*Capitol Square Review and Advisory Bd. v. Pinette* 1995). Though the hostility towards Youmans's crossing of the color-line was formidable, he found some support from the chancellor of his university, who encouraged him on his entry into the Alpha brotherhood (Parks 2000).

Throughout subsequent years, college-educated white young women and men continued to pledge Black Greek-letter organizations (BGLOs). While Asian and Latino individuals also began pledging BGLOs, their entry was not documented to the same regard. Asian and Latino BGLO membership is not without controversy, but it is white members whose racial transgression most acutely embodies the U.S.' history of racial subjection of Black people. Overall, cross-racial membership in Black fraternities and sororities still draws confusion, objection, and mystification.

In 2016, the issue of whites in Black fraternities garnered mainstream attention when white Kappa Alpha Psi member Sam White achieved social media fame as a video of him shimmying, a signature Kappa dance move, went viral. TMZ entertainment news, which typically features short, impromptu on-the-street interviews with celebrities, even ran a short segment on White with the title "Kappa Alpha Psi Member Sam White: Coolest White Guy Alive?" (TMZ 2016). The interview with White was featured during the TMZ Live television show, where TMZ reporters gather in the newsroom to discuss the most entertaining or potentially popular interviews. At the end of the segment, reporter Van Lathan jokingly suggested that they should ask him this question to find out if he is really white: "Did O.J. Simpson do it?" *The People vs. OJ Simpson*, a short television series chronicling the infamous, high-profile 1990s court case,[1] had recently concluded. Although Simpson was acquitted, public opinion regarding his guilt was, and still is, split along racial lines with Black Americans largely claiming his innocence and white Americans his guilt. Before revealing White's answer, the host reminds us, "He's living in two different worlds. He's the coolest white guy alive but he is in fact white." In less than a minute and a half, the total duration of the segment on White, the racial expectations of White are laid forth – that in joining a Black fraternity he has to give up some of his 'whiteness' and although his affiliation with Blackness may provide him some level of cultural cachet, "he is in fact white" and therefore may still be joined to certain beliefs that cannot be overcome. In the end, White answered with, "I'm gonna go with a strong no comment."

While the TMZ segment was a lighthearted clip capitalizing on the peculiarity of this modern-day color-line transgression, non-Black entrance into BGLOs continues to be contentious. From the first instance of a non-Black pledge in the 1940s through the continued presence of non-Black members, while "there's been no rush for Whites to join Black organizations" or for other non-Black members for that matter (*Ebony Magazine* 2000:176), the ongoing presence of these racial boundary transgressors in this Black space raises questions around the meaning of race and the nature of race relations.

As the examples of Levin, Youmans, and White suggest, non-Black members of BGLOs are racial curiosities. How and why, then, do non-Blacks come to identify with and dedicate themselves to BGLO membership? In this book, we explore this modern-day form of color-line crossing from the perspective of white, Asian, and Latino BGLO members. These members express their cross-racial affiliation in a very public manner by pledging Black organizations that are imbued with Black cultural traditions and symbols. How do non-Black members negotiate their racial identity as they pledge their hearts, minds, and strength[2] to Black-created, Black-led, and Black-focused organizations? We reveal how BGLO membership leads to the bolstering, blurring, or broadening of their racial identities. At the same time, we analyze the limitations of individual-level challenges to larger racial ideologies and practices.

Crossing the Line

In the spring of 2004, the University of Memphis' Epsilon Epsilon Chapter of Alpha Kappa Alpha Sorority, Incorporated admitted its first Asian American member: Wendy. As one might expect, her membership in the first Black sorority, founded at Howard University in 1908, was met with mixed reactions. There were those who found her desire for membership acceptable, and those who were offended by the presence of a racial outsider in a decidedly Black sisterhood. In fact, the night before her initiation, an older chapter member called her to ask if she was sure this was what she wanted to do. Since her own experience with a rocky initiation into Alpha Kappa Alpha Sorority, Incorporated, Wendy was curious about the experiences of other non-Black members. She only knew of a couple other non-Black members from attending regional step show competitions and regional sorority conferences, and within those events, she did not see any others. While she understood what her membership meant to her and those around her, she wanted to know how other non-Black BGLO members made meaning out of their cross-racial membership.

In 2010, Devon worked as a white family therapy intern in a Native American-specific mental health agency in the Pacific Northwest with a predominantly Native clientele, which offered many traditional Native healing techniques. A white therapist working with Native American clients was not always accepted. Many in the community felt uncomfortable with a white person taking a position of relative power over Native clients, as well as having concerns about if Devon should have access to the knowledge of Native healing traditions. This role made Devon reflect upon the role of racial "outsiders" within racialized groups and organizations. She has focused her research on how individuals cross the color-line. In her most recent project, she is investigating the experiences of and tensions around white students at historically Black colleges and universities, a population that closely mirrors the dynamics of non-Black BGLO members. Given her own experience within a cross-racial organization, Devon wanted to understand the practices of others who also have crossed the color-line in such a stark way.

We bring these unique experiences as racial "outsiders" to examining the experiences of non-Black BGLO members. Wendy's status as a member of a Black sorority brought the knowledge and connections that were essential to navigating and accessing a small and often ignored population. Not being a member of a BGLO allowed Devon to have an outsider's perspective and permitted new questions. These experiences together allowed the authors to have both an "insider" and "outsider" approach to the study of BGLOs.

The problem of the color-line has been pointed to as the central concern of our time (Du Bois 1903). The "color-line" refers to the persistent racial segregation, both legalized and informal, that exists within the United States. Racially divided social spaces allow a window into the contested, uneasy, and politicized feelings around the color-line. Integration and racial diversity have been hailed as integral to the progression of a racially just society. In an era often exalted as moving toward "colorblindness," many believe that the existence of social spaces of color represents a racially-based blight on our otherwise "post-racial" society. On the other hand, however, there is a different perspective, in which racial spaces provide much needed support and solidarity to marginalized groups in society. We explore the tensions between these two perspectives as they apply to the entrance of non-black members into Black fraternities and sororities.

Setting the Stage: Race and Higher Education

More than 60 years after the milestone ruling of *Brown v. Board of Education* (1954) in which racial segregation in public schools was found unconstitutional, education remains a battleground for the accumulation and distribution of racialized resources. In higher education specifically, profound racial disparities between college graduation rates remain. Given the many economic and social advantages awarded to those with a college degree, access to and successful completion of higher education for people of color stands as an important venue for allowing people of color access to resourced networks and the potential for economic gains. Additionally, racial diversity on campus has been linked to enhanced positive college experiences for all students on campus (Jayakumar 2008; Mitchell 2001). Accordingly, colleges and universities across the country have been subject to calls to bolster campus racial diversity through increased admission of students of color, as well as retention efforts aimed at creating a campus environment welcoming of a diverse student body (Bowen and Bok 2000).

Despite these pushes for a diverse student body, pernicious race-related incidents on campus persist, including racist-themed parties featuring white students dressed up like Blacks, Native Americans, Latinos, or Asians, the placement of nooses hung from trees or around statues of Black alumni, racial profiling by campus police, and the defacement of school property with racial epithets. Many students of color describe a continued sense of fear and alienation on college campuses (McCabe 2009). These racially charged incidents raise questions about higher education's approach to racial diversity. Mirroring earlier decades of student activism, throughout 2015, 2016, and 2017 students across the U.S. staged demonstrations and walkouts to protest racism on their college campuses. Lists of demands from Concerned Student 1950 (University of Missouri), the Black Justice League (Princeton), People of Color at Ithaca (Ithaca College), CMCers of Color (Claremont McKenna College), and similar others outlined the lack of meaningful attention to racist policies, practices, or incidents at their respective schools. Together these demonstrations underscore the futility of promotional racial diversity without multi-level engagement with the history, power relations, and material manifestations of race, or what we describe as 'weak' diversity. Stemming from 1980s multiculturalism, which celebrated cultural differences while also promoting assimilation, 'weak' diversity effectively undercuts attempts to acknowledge and address racial disparities.

As this wave of student activism reminds us, schools are not just places to learn course material and gain academic credentials. Colleges and universities are also spaces where students learn about their place in society – whether through the types of courses taught, the guest speakers invited to campus, the resources available to different student groups, or the types of students, groups and activities that are policed. In sum, the college campus both reflects and perpetuates a hierarchy of belonging based on race.

In response to racism experienced on college campuses, students of color often create specific organizations for people of color as safe havens to cope with campus racial microaggressions, racial discrimination, and isolation (Solorzano et al. 2000). These campus organizations, such as ethnic or cultural clubs, Black student unions, or racial justice groups, act as "counter-spaces" that intend to provide students reprieve from the dominance of whiteness throughout the rest of their college experiences. Racial and ethnic-specific organizations have been shown to provide students of color the opportunity to express and develop their racial identities, provide opportunities to engage in community service activities, advocate for their ethnic communities via institutional change, and connect with other students of their racial group (Museus 2008).

One such entity is that of Black Greek-letter organizations. BGLOs were founded in the early 1900s towards the goal of empowering the Black community. By our best estimates from membership information on BGLO national websites, there are over 1.25 million BGLO members and over 6,300 BGLO chapters worldwide. Although most non-Black individuals may be initially unfamiliar with BGLOs, many high-profile Black celebrities, activists, and scholars are members of the organizations, including Dr. Martin Luther King, Jr., Thurgood Marshall, Toni Morrison, Shaquille O'Neal, Wanda Sykes, and Omari Hardwick. Since their establishment, BGLOs have remained a mainstay on both historically Black and predominantly white campuses alike, acting as a specific type of counter-space. On predominantly white campuses, they provide Black students with a space to develop Black friendships, access deep networks of chapter and organizational alumni, and engage in meaningful service to the Black community. On historically Black campuses, they dovetail with the larger agenda of racial justice and engaging in community service targeted at bettering the Black community.

Why Study Non-Black BGLO Members?

BGLOs are characterized by continued community service, academic excellence, lifelong membership, and an extensive pledging process prior to official membership (Hughey 2007). As such, existing BGLO research largely focuses on either the benefits of membership or the problems associated with pledging, particularly hazing. Benefits from BGLO membership are wide-ranging, and include the ability to assume inter-organizational leadership roles and develop leadership skills (Kimbrough 1995); social support for Black students, particularly at predominantly white colleges and universities (McClure 2006; Patton and Bonner 2001); racial and gender identity development (Harper and Quaye 2007); and can enhance educational engagement inside the college classroom (Harper 2008).

Although BGLOs have always been majority-Black organizations, there have been small numbers of non-Black individuals pledging membership to the organizations (Hughey 2007). We argue that these non-Black members of BGLOs are a unique and powerful instance of cross-racial relationships and interactions that are different from other types of cross-racial memberships in Greek life. That is, unlike predominantly white Greek organizations, where the racial agendas are covert and hidden, Black fraternities and sororities are explicitly organized as an avenue for Black individuals to advance the Black community.

Given the centrality of Blackness in the organizations that are premised on notions of Black community strength and uplift, the entrance of these non-Black individuals into BGLOs offers an interesting case to understand how cross-racial relationships function within contemporary U.S. society. In an era with both heightened racial tensions, as evidenced through the controversy of the Black Lives Matter movement, and the prevailing notion that race no longer impacts life chances, as demonstrated through the push to be "colorblind," non-Black members who join Black social organizations provide rare insights into how racial relations, racial identities, and ideas about race function within this paradox (Bonilla-Silva 2009).

Although academic scholarship on BGLOs has been increasing in recent years, substantial gaps and misunderstandings in the academic knowledge about the organizations persist, signaling the need for more work (McClure 2006). In particular, there is limited research that systematically explores the experiences of non-Black BGLO members. This lack of attention to cross-racial BGLO membership is troubling not only because of a need to add knowledge about this unique group of members, but also because of the essential and tangible issues regarding the purpose and survival of Black fraternities and sororities that non-Black members illuminate.

The existence of non-Black BGLO members highlight conundrums about the potential for cross-racial membership in Black organizations to dissolve the importance of Blackness that these fraternities and sororities were founded on in the first place. That is, is there a tipping point where there would be too many non-Black BGLO members for the organizations to retain their original purpose of building up the Black community? Studying the organizational response to non-Black members aids in answering this question, drawing essential conclusions about how Black fraternities and sororities can continue to thrive in the contemporary era. Additionally, these insights about how organizations are impacted when individuals join who may challenge or change the original intent of the groups are transferable to many other present-day issues such as trans men at women's colleges, straight allies in LGBT groups or establishments, and white students at historically Black colleges and universities.

Therefore, we believe that non-Black BGLO members are uniquely positioned to answer questions such as: What motivates non-Black BGLO members to cross the color-line in such a stark and noticeable way? What are the experiences of non-Black members in fraternities and sororities organized around Blackness? How does the study of non-Black BGLO members contribute to our understanding of the significance of race, identity, and group boundaries in the contemporary U.S.?

Our approach is distinguished from the extant literature in two main ways. First, the BGLO members who participated in previous studies generally identify as Black, meaning that very few of these studies discuss non-Black BGLO members. Second, those studies that do acknowledge or investigate cross-racial membership often focus mainly on racial identity and ideology. Our study is unique in that while it adds to the literature on racial identities and ideologies, it also takes into account the outcomes and benefits of membership. Moreover, many of the studies that consider non-Black BGLO membership do so by only studying white members and experiences of Black Greek life. Our study is different in that it considers the experiences of a number of racially and ethnically diverse BGLO members. Our data, therefore, aid in building a more robust picture of the organizational impact of non-Black membership.

To do so, we utilize a theoretical framework that centers on understanding the consequences of breaching racial boundaries. Racial integration is often considered a crucial step towards achieving racial justice in U.S. society. The premise of the goal of racial integration is built upon the theory that increased cross-racial contact leads to improved cross-racial relations, known as contact theory (Allport 1954). The conditions under which the contact occurs has been the subject of much debate (Mullen et al. 1992; Pettigrew 1998; Riordan 1978; Stephan 1987). Whereas Allport suggested that equal status, common goals, cooperation, and support of authorities were essential for the contact hypothesis to be successful, other research has found these conditions unnecessary (Pettigrew and Tropp 2006). Instead, social psychologists argue that contact, aside from dangerous or threatening behavior, will promote tolerance and positive reception (Pettigrew and Tropp 2006; Pettigrew 2008; Stephan and White Stephan 1985). Given the intimate conditions of Greek organizations, contact theory would seem to be most successful in this context.

However, contact theory assumes that cross-racial contact will be enough to challenge and disrupt entrenched racial ideas and patterns. Studies of symbolic boundaries, on the other hand, explain how and why identity-based divisions between people become meaningful. Symbolic boundaries are used to classify people and justify hierarchical relationships, and may provide answers as to why racial contact may not be enough to further positive racial relations (Lamont and Fournier 1992; Small et al. 2010). Therefore, by combining these two theories, we are able to provide insight into both the enabling and constraining influence of racial boundary crossing in Black Greek organizations. Throughout the book, we utilize both contact theory and symbolic boundaries to understand the impact of non-Black BGLO membership on members' ideas of race, their racial identities, and the organizations themselves.

Research Design and Approach

Given the unique experiences of non-Black BGLO members, they seem poised to answer questions about organizational practices, racial hierarchy, and racial identity. Accordingly, in this book we concentrate on the experiences and outcomes of non-Black BGLO members. Between 2014 and 2015, we conducted in-depth interviews with 34 non-Black BGLO members. As we were interested in non-Black individuals' experiences in BGLOs, and because Black multiracial people are often racialized as Black, we limited the criteria to exclude Black multiracial BGLO members.

While the peculiarity of their membership makes non-Black members hypervisible, the rarity of non-Black members made finding participants challenging. In the end, the members we talked with were found through mutual networks or referred by other interview participants. As such, this book does not represent fully the experience of all non-Black BGLO members. However, the shared patterns of experience and approach to crossing the color-line herein are illustrative of processes in broader society. Wendy's shared status as a non-Black member likely facilitated our respondents' participation in the study while at the same time inhibiting others. In addition to the difficulty in identifying this population of BGLO members, there was likely hesitancy from some non-Black members given the relative secrecy surrounding BGLO membership and membership processes. Additionally, as one potential respondent, who declined to participate, explained, he felt he was not qualified to discuss his experiences because he had only recently become a member of his fraternity. This certainly did not stop other members who had recently joined their BGLO from participating in the study, but it may point to the difference in experiences that this non-Black member had in contrast to those who did agree to share their stories. As you will find within the chapters that follow, while most of our members experienced some level of backlash, they were able to make sense of those experiences in a way that enabled them still to feel like full members of their organization. It is likely that those non-Black members who were not able to integrate their less welcoming experiences chose not to participate in our study.

One unique feature of BGLOs is the continued and expected post-collegiate involvement of members. Therefore, eligible participants included non-Black BGLO members regardless of when they became members of their respective organization. The inclusion of respondents who were post-undergraduate allowed us to capture the continued importance of BGLO membership to members' understanding of race, race relations, and racial stratification. Although approximately two-thirds of our final sample was post-college, each of them identified their undergraduate college experiences as a salient turning point in how they thought about race and their place with in a racialized society. Further, the majority of respondents maintained some substantive level of active engagement with their organizations at either the local or national level, in many cases both, regardless of their initial date of membership.

We approached these non-Black BGLO members with the goal of understanding their experiences around a number of topics, including their motivation for membership in a BGLO, how they conceived of the meaning of their membership, how they understood the importance of race and the prevalence of discrimination, how their friends outside their organization and their family members responded to their membership, and how they understood their own racial identity. Our interview questions were therefore designed to respond to the literature on social boundaries, racial identity development, and the influence of group membership on experiences of race and discrimination. We also gathered an array of demographic information, including the racial demographics and racial integration within respondents' childhood neighborhoods, primary and secondary schools, and college campuses, the previous cross-racial membership in their BGLO chapter, and their socioeconomic status.

Of the 34 non-Black BGLO members we spoke to, 13 of the respondents identified as white, ten as Asian American, six as Latino/a, and five as multiracial (see the Methodological Appendix for more details on demographics). Ages ranged from 20 to 44, with a median age of 29.5. Respondents represented eight of the nine organizations under the National Pan-Hellenic Council. Though virtually all respondents reported being involved in their BGLO through community service or maintaining ties with members, approximately three-fourths of respondents (74 percent; $n=25$) reported that they are currently financially active at the national level. Maintaining annual dues to the BGLO's national body is the cornerstone of membership. Membership dues enable BGLOs to continue racial uplift projects in cities and states throughout the U.S. and in communities abroad.[3] Some 19 respondents (56 percent) reported that they had held or currently hold a leadership position in their BGLO. At the time of the interview, all respondents held membership in their fraternity or sorority for at least one semester. Length of membership ranged from one semester to over 24 years. In total, the members possessed 259 years of experience in BGLOs.

Who Are Non-Black BGLO Members?

Although there are longstanding debates about the presence of non-Black BGLO members in Black Greek organizations, the overall number of non-Black members is relatively small. There are no official numbers on the percentage of cross-racial membership, but it is rare for there to be more than a couple of non-Black members in any given BGLO chapter, if at all. Non-Black members, though hyper-visible within their BGLOs, at regional and national BGLO conferences, and within the Black community of their college campuses, are virtually invisible to the general public. A majority of non-Black individuals have no knowledge of Black fraternities and sororities. In fact, only about 20 percent of our respondents reported any awareness of BGLOs prior to entering college, and only 5 percent of those respondents expressed that they had some interest in joining a Black Greek organization prior to coming to college.

Take Kelly, a 42-year-old white Black Greek-letter sorority member, for example. Neither of her parents attended college and although her older sister did, she was not involved in Greek life. As a result, Kelly had no knowledge of sororities and fraternities, white or Black. She would learn about BGLOs through her co-workers at her university who were BGLO members. Kelly found a connection to the Christian values of her sorority, and the deep and ongoing commitment to community service based in the history of the organization.

While the small number of non-Black members share an identification with BGLOs, there are few other factors or traits that they share. Our respondents were raised in states across the U.S., though the majority (about 70 percent) was from the South and Southeast, from Arkansas to Georgia, Florida, and North Carolina. The rest were from the Southwest, the West Coast, the Northeast, and the Midwest. This concentration in the South largely maps onto where BGLO chapters are most frequently found.

Our respondents had a range of pre-college experiences with racial diversity. About half of our respondents described their upbringing as taking place in a diverse area comprising of two or more racial and ethnic groups different from their own, nine respondents reported that their hometown was predominantly Black, and nine lived in predominantly white areas both rural and suburban. Similarly, whereas some members did not meet a non-white person until their undergraduate years, others reported participating in racial diversity programs, having predominantly Black friendship circles, and attending white anti-racist workshops prior to college.

For example, Osita, a 33-year-old Latina Black Greek-letter sorority member, grew up in racially diverse communities and attended racially diverse schools. She experienced a "culture shock" attending college because of the lack of diversity on her campus; there were very few Latino or Black students. She described her experience, stating, "I oftentimes was the token Latino." Her older sister had joined a historically white sorority, but Osita shared that she knew that type of organization was not for her based on her own interests, circle of friends, and the types of activities she liked. Osita stated: "That wasn't something that I felt aligned with who I was and my cultural identity."

For college, where the majority of respondents first learned about BGLOs, respondents attended both public and private institutions, with both being about equally represented. The majority of colleges attended were large with over 100,000 students enrolled and in an urban or suburban area. The racial diversity of their college campuses ranged from having multiple racial and ethnic groups represented, to those having only a small handful of non-white students. Only one of the campuses included historically Asian or Latino sororities or fraternities, and only one of the campuses included a multiracial sorority.

Keilana, a 28-year-old Laotian sorority member, who attended a large, public university in the South, described her college campus as predominantly white with a small Black student body. She grew up in a working-class neighborhood, in a household where English was not the first language, and where she and her brothers were raised in the cultural and religious traditions of her Asian ethnic community. She was one of the few from her hometown neighborhood to attend college. Keilana described how she did not really understand what it meant to be successful in college, but through a timely intervention from the director of her work-study job at the campus multicultural center, she became connected to a core group of high-achieving, highly involved students of color, most of whom were members of BGLOs. Through relationships with her BGLO peers and participation in their community service activities, Keilana found an important connection to her college women peers and the work they were doing in the community.

Book Overview

In the pages that follow, we find that our respondents are unique in that their membership in a BGLO forces them to confront the saliency of the color-line in ways that many other students are able to avoid or ignore. We argue that these experiences of non-Black BGLO members not only demonstrate the continued significance of race on the college campus, but also the complexity around racial identity and group membership. Although higher education is often espoused as an equalizer among racial groups, we find that racial divides continue to shape students' experiences and on-campus groups' material resources. To do this, we highlight how non-Black memberships influence campus racial climate, racial identity and understanding, and outcomes beyond college.

In Chapter 1, we provide a historical view of Black fraternities and sororities. In order to conceptualize the impact and experiences of non-Black members, we trace the route of BGLOs from their foundations as associations that provided an alternative to the segregated white fraternity system, which barred non-white memberships, to their contemporary place on the college campus. We provide an account of how BGLOs relate to other Black organizations and associations, such as the Black church and Black secret societies. We then discuss the research on non-black BGLO members in order to highlight the similarities and differences with our particular respondents.

In Chapter 2, we investigate BGLOs as a site of identity development. We begin by exploring the different ways that non-Black members originally approached their membership to a Black fraternity or sorority. We document four ways that respondents expressed their approaches to joining and participating in a BGLO as a non-black member: colorblind crossing (in which race was seen as unimportant or as a distasteful reason for joining), careful crossing (in which respondents recognized that they were crossing a color-line and wished to proceed cautiously), challenging by crossing (wherein respondents characterized their membership as an intentional desire to break down racial barriers), and collective crossing (wherein respondents of color felt categorized within a larger Black racial category and joined as a response to this classification). We also document how BGLOs facilitate both racial and gender identity development, and increase non-Black members' understanding of racism writ large, as well as racism against Blacks, specifically.

In Chapter 3, we explore the relationship between context and social boundaries by showing how campus racial climate influences how racial boundaries are drawn and contested. We found that the racial climate on campus acts as a central catalyst for membership in race-based organizations. That is, both white and non-white non-Black BGLO members sought out Black fraternities and sororities in response to a racially divided campus climate. In so doing, non-Black BGLO members establish a collective identity that positions them as more similar to their Black brothers and sisters than the broader white college campus. However, this same membership also creates problems when non-Black members are challenged or questioned within their organization regarding their own racial group membership.

In Chapter 4, we illuminate the impact of sustained lifelong bonds of brotherhood and sisterhood on non-Black members. We find that non-Black members characterized their experiences in their fraternities and sororities as having lasting impacts beyond their college years. In particular, our respondents noted that the skills that they learned in BGLOs transferred to increased self-esteem and self-confidence, transformed their career choices, and provided them with the knowledge to succeed in a variety of workplaces. Membership also affected non-Black members' relationships with their family, particularly around how they communicated about racism and race with family members.

We conclude with an overview of the analysis of our findings. We then discuss the implications of color-line crossing, like non-Blacks entering BGLOs, for broader race relations.

Notes

1 O.J. Simpson, a Black former National Football League (NFL) player, was tried on two counts of murder for the death of his ex-wife, Nicole Brown Simpson, and her friend, Ron Goldman, who were both white. The case became a cultural touchstone for racial tensions, with the defense arguing that Simpson was framed by racist police officers.
2 Most BGLOs have organizational songs, chants, or membership rituals that include pledging one's heart and strength to the organization or that characterize the organization as holding a sacred place in their hearts.
3 Among BGLO members, there is debate over the legitimacy of one's membership if one is not financially active. By one estimate, only one in ten fraternity initiates and four in ten sorority initiates remain financially active (Ross 2010).

References

Allport, Gordon W. 1954. *The Nature of Prejudice*. Reading, MA: Addison-Wesley.

Bonilla-Silva, Eduardo. 2009. *Racism Without Racists: Color-Blind Racism and the Persistence of Inequality in America*, 3rd Ed. New York, NY: Rowman & Littlefield Publishers.

Bowen, William G., and Derek Bok. 2000. *The Shape of the River*. Princeton, NJ: Princeton University Press.

Capitol Square Review and Advisory Board, et al. Petitioners v. Vincent J. Pinette, Donnie A. Carr, and Knights of the Ku Klux Klan. 1995. 515 U.S. 753, 770–771.

Du Bois, W.E.B. 1903. *The Souls of Black Folk*. Chicago: A. C. McClurg & Co.

Ebony Magazine. 1946a. "Negro Frat Admits 'White Brother.'" *Ebony Magazine* 1(11):24–25.

Ebony Magazine. 1946b. "Foes of Admission of Whites to Alpha Defeated in Fight on Interracialism." *Ebony Magazine* 1(11):26.

Ebony Magazine. 2000. "Whites in Black Sororities and Fraternities." *Ebony Magazine* LVI(2):172–176.

Harper, Shaun R. 2008. "The Effects of Sorority and Fraternity Membership on Class Participation and African American Student Engagement in Predominantly White Classroom Environments." *College Student Affairs Journal* 27(1):94–115.

Harper, Shaun R. and Stephen John Quaye. 2007. "Student Organizations as Venues for Black Identity Expression and Development among African American Male Student Leaders." *Journal of College Student Development* 48(2):127–144.

Hughey, Matthew W. 2007. "Crossing the Sands, Crossing the Color Line: Non-Black Members of Black Greek Letter Organizations." *Journal of African American Studies* 11(1):55–75.

Jayakumar, Uma. 2008. "Can Higher Education Meet the Needs of an Increasingly Diverse and Global Society? Campus Diversity and Cross-Cultural Workforce Competencies." *Harvard Educational Review* 78(4):615–651.

Kimbrough, Walter M. 1995. "Self-assessment, Participation, and Value of Leadership Skills, Activities, and Experiences for Black Students Relative to their Membership in Historically Black Fraternities and Sororities." *Journal of Negro Education* 64(1):63–74.

Lamont, Michele, and Marcel Fournier. 1992. "Introduction." Pp. 1–16 in *Cultivating Differences: Symbolic Boundaries and the Making of Inequality*, edited by Michele Lamont and Marcel Fournier. Chicago: University of Chicago Press.

McCabe, Janice. 2009. "Racial and Gender Microaggressions on a Predominantly-White Campus: Experiences of Black, Latina/o and White Undergraduates." *Race, Gender, & Class* 16(1/2):133–151.

McClure, Stephanie M. 2006. "Voluntary Association Membership: Black Greek Men on a Predominantly White Campus." *The Journal of Higher Education* 77(6):1037–1057.

Mitchell, Chang J. 2001. "The Positive Educational Effects of Racial Diversity on Campus." Pp. 175–186 in *Diversity Challenged: Evidence on the Impact of Affirmative Action*, by G. Orfield (ed). Cambridge, MA: Harvard Education Publishing Group.

Mullen, Brian, Rupert Brown, and Colleen Smith. 1992. "Ingroup Bias as a Function of Salience, Relevance, and Status: An Integration." *European Journal of Social Psychology* 22:103–122.

Museus, Samuel D. 2008. "The Role of Ethnic Student Organizations in Fostering African American and Asian American Students' Cultural Adjustment and Membership at Predominantly White Institutions." *Journal of College Student Development* 49(6):568–586.

Olive Brown, et al. v. Board of Education of Topeka, et al. 1954. 347 U.S. 483.

Parks, Gregory S. 2000. "The Alpha Experience from the 'Minority' Perspective." *The Sphinx* 85:40–43.

Patton, Lori D. and Fred Bonner, II. 2001. "Advising the Historically Black Greek Letter Organization: A Reason for Angst or Euphoria?" *NASAP Journal* 4:17–30.

Pettigrew, Thomas F. 1998. "Intergroup Contact Theory." *Annual Review of Psychology* 49:65–85.

Pettigrew, Thomas F. 2008. "Future Directions for Intergroup Contact Theory and Research." *International Journal of Intercultural Relations* 32:187–199.

Pettigrew, Thomas F. and Linda R. Tropp. 2006. "A Meta-analytic Test of Intergroup Contact Theory." *Journal of Personality and Social Psychology* 90:751–783.

Riordan, Cornelius. 1978. "Equal-Status Interracial Contact: A Review and Revision of the Concept." *International Journal of Intercultural Relations* 11:143–154.

Ross, Lawrence. 2010. "Frats and Sorors in Name Only? You Might Need to Get Dropped." TheRoot.com, September 1. Retrieved from www.theroot.com/blog/the-divine-nine/inactive_black_greeks_might_need_to_lose_their_rights/.

Small, Mario Luis, David J. Harding, and Michele Lamont. 2010. "Reconsidering Culture and Poverty." *The ANNALS of American Academy of Political and Social Science* 629:6–27.

Solorzano, Daniel, Miguel Ceja, and Tara Yosso. 2000. "Critical Race Theory, Racial Microaggressions, and Campus Racial Climate: The Experiences of African American College Students." *The Journal of Negro Education* 69(1/2):60–73.

Stephan, Walter G. 1987. "The Contact Hypothesis in Intergroup Relations." *Review of Personality and Social Psychology* 9:13–40.

Stephan, Walter G., and Cookie White Stephan. 1985. "Intergroup Anxiety" *Journal of Social Issues* 41:157–175.

TMZ. 2016. "Kappa Alpha Psi Member Sam White: Coolest White Guy Alive?" TMZ TV. April 10. Retrieved from www.youtube.com/watch?v=XgyCdBGDaU4.

1

BROTHERHOOD AND SISTERHOOD

What Are Black Greek-Letter Organizations?

On a Friday afternoon during her first semester of undergrad, Wendy took her usual seat by the window in her philosophy class. As she and her classmates discussed Frantz Fanon, the excited sounds of shouting, applause, and then the syncopated rhythms of a yard show drifted into the room. One of the Black Greek-letter organizations' (BGLOs) Greek Weeks was coming to a close. As is customary on college campuses with BGLO chapters, throughout the semester, each chapter has a week dedicated to showcasing their organization. Chapters create elaborate themes for the weeks, with each day highlighting the programmatic thrusts of their respective organizations. For example, a week may be themed around old school hip-hop with each day titled after a well-known hip-hop song coupled with one of the BGLO's community service activities, or around a popular movie with each day organized around a quote from the movie paired with a racial justice action. The close of the week culminates with the chapter having a yard show. At a yard show, chapter members perform choreographed step routines, strolls, and chants in front of an audience of the campus's other BGLO chapter members, fellow BGLO members from nearby campuses who travel to see the show as well as the campus's Black student community. The allure of the yard show is simple – showmanship, sportsmanship, and solidarity. There is pride in seeing fellow BGLO members from your particular organization 'run the yard.' There is the general camaraderie among BGLO members regardless of the specific organization being highlighted. Then, there is the feeling of campus belonging for Black students, both BGLO members and non-members alike, which is atypical for their everyday campus experience. Wendy, the unknowing freshman, had unwittingly scheduled a class during the most important on-campus social time of the week. Like many other students, she ended up skipping those Friday classes during a Greek Week. Better to miss a few classes than to miss a yard show.

This scene is not unlike the excitement that surrounds Black fraternities and sororities at college campuses across the country. From step shows, signing, roll calls, and community service initiatives, BGLOs are thick with tradition that not only provides members with a sense of belonging, but also acts as a spectacle for non-members on many campuses. Moreover, BGLOs and their activities are often the center of the Black community at majority-white institutions. Given the role of contemporary BGLOs, what is their history?

In this chapter, we examine the historical and contemporary status of Black Greek-letter organizations from their early years as vehicles for community uplift to their place in the current system of higher education. Understanding the role of BGLOs in the Black community helps to contextualize the experiences of the BGLO members that we document in later chapters, especially as it relates to their membership as non-Black individuals. After an exploration of how Black fraternal organizations birthed BGLOs and aided them in developing into the current organizations that exist today, we discuss the research on non-Black BGLO members.

Foundations of Black Fraternal Organizations

Black race-based organizations trace back to the social activism and community identity of religious institutions. Black autonomous churches began to take shape during times of slavery and early American settlement, during which slaves were socially divided due to different ethnicities, traditions, and languages from their origins (Lincoln and Mamiya 1990). The church aided in helping to break down these differences and acted as a unifying force. After the emancipation from slavery in 1863, these Black churches became formalized outside of the institution of slavery and began to provide a resource for the formation of Black schools and workspaces in a time of depravity of resources for Black people (Billingsley 1999).

Black churches became the expected and assumed centers for racial uplift, as complete freedom for Blacks implied not only social and political freedom, but also moral and religious freedom (Ross 2003). Therefore, parishioners relied on ministers and church members to take public stands against lynching, discrimination, and segregation. Despite this, prominent Black leaders questioned the ultimate success that the Black church could have in securing political and social rights for Blacks due to its religious focus (Warnock 2014). Additionally, cracks and fissures within the Black community began to form, made emblematic by the move to more insular and elite Black churches in some parts of the country (Moore 1999). As Eric Lincoln and Lawrence Mamiya (1990:9) state, "Some of the more astute and visionary church leaders saw the need to develop secular vehicles in order to cope with more complex and pluralistic urban environments." It was out of this skepticism that other venues for racial uplift were founded, which led to race-based organizations in other facets of social life.

The legacies of slavery, racism, and segregation obstructed the possibility for civic cooperation between Blacks and whites. Central facets of social life, such as fraternal and civic organizations, excluded Blacks from membership. Additionally, Blacks were barred from full participation in trade unionism and electoral politics. This exclusion denied the opportunity to experience the ideals of shared citizenship, professional networking and potential business ventures, and develop connections across regional and state lines (Skocpol et al. 2006).

Black organizations, particularly civic organizations, began to spring up as a viable alternative to the predominantly white organizations that had been exclusive. These Black non-religious organizations became the second largest and most extensive sector of social organization next to churches. Fraternal groups allowed Black men the opportunities to gain valuable business and professional experiences, such as networking and leadership skills. They also provided a venue for Black women to engage in charity work for Black communities, allowing for the honing of their leadership skills and creating an opportunity to bond with other Black women (Moore 1999). In doing so, they became vital hubs of civil and political causes, such as advocating for Black politicians and for Black civil rights. Additionally, Black fraternal groups provided resources that the state did not, including life and funeral insurance to their members, as well as financial aid to economically needy families within their communities.

In addition to providing economically to their members, race-based organizations also provided racial uplift to their community. Racial uplift emphasizes the importance of community building to realize an inclusive vision of Black advancement through the work of institutions such as race-based organizations (Ross 2003). Racial uplift was, in more recent history, personified within the notion of the "Talented Tenth," popularized by W.E.B. Du Bois (1903), who suggested that the top 10 percent of the Black race would serve to uplift the remaining 90 percent of the Black community onto equal footing with whites. Therefore, race-based organizations served as spaces that provided both material and cultural resources to communities that have been historically underserved and ignored within the mainstream.

While providing racial uplift was the core of Black organizations ranging from benevolent societies to churches, Black secret societies were unique in their structure and organization (Hughey 2013). Black secret societies, such as the Prince Hall Free and Accepted Masons, Grand United Order of Odd Fellows, and Improved Benevolent Protective Order of the Elks of the World, offered similar community uplift activities as benevolent societies but were differentiated by their male-only membership and secrecy (Butler 2012). These organizations were created to form and maintain long-lasting ties among their members, address racial exclusion from white fraternal organizations and society at large, and racial uplift. Characterized by restrictive membership and secret rituals, Black secret societies maintained a structure that allowed for the perpetuation of their organization and community impact (Butler 2012). Their organizational structure included local chapters, regional areas, and a national governing body. The influence of these Black secret societies can be seen in the structure and scope of Black Greek-letter organizations.

The Beginnings of BGLOs

One of the primary sites for race-based organizations and institutions was education, in which historically Black colleges developed in the late 1800s as alternatives to primarily white colleges that had denied admission to Black American students due to segregation policies (Whaley 2009). These historically Black colleges were often the only educational avenue for Blacks until the early twentieth century. However, in the early 1900s, a number of white schools had begun to admit small numbers of Black students. Accordingly, a number of elite Blacks chose to attend these colleges as opposed to Black centers of education as a "degree from a predominantly white school was ultimately preferable to any other" (Moore 1999:113). However, very few Blacks, even among the elite, were able to attend predominantly white schools in the North, leading to a small population of Blacks at these elite institutions. As these populations began to grow and students began to connect based on their similar experiences, Black students established Black student organizations (Moore 1999).

BGLOs were founded in the early twentieth century as a response to the racial exclusion policies that existed in white Greek-letter organizations' constitutions and the general ostracism Black students faced on historically white college campuses. In order to combat academic pressures and racial isolation, Black students formed social and study groups that eventually were established as national fraternities. The first was Alpha Phi Alpha, which was founded at Cornell University in 1906. Although originating as a literacy society with the goal of the retention of Black male students, the group adopted the name Alpha Phi Alpha and set course to establish themselves as a fraternity (Wesley 1995). This change in scope signaled their desire to create a more permanent organization that would be recognized by Cornell University. The first national Black collegiate sorority quickly followed suit, with Alpha Kappa Alpha being established in 1908 at Howard University. Although Alpha Kappa Alpha's founders did not experience the racial exclusion at Howard that Alpha Phi Alpha's members did at Cornell, Alpha Kappa Alpha founders encountered conservative politics at Howard that discouraged radical activism and explicit expression of African cultural elements (Whaley 2010). Furthermore, Alpha Kappa Alpha founders' experiences as Black women reflected a distinct raced and gendered position.

Over the next 14 years, six additional fraternities and sororities were founded: Kappa Alpha Psi (1911, Indiana University), Omega Psi Phi (1911, Howard University), Delta Sigma Theta (1913, Howard University), Phi Beta Sigma

(1914, Howard University), Zeta Phi Beta (1920, Howard University), and Sigma Gamma Rho (1922, Butler University). Kappa Alpha Psi and Sigma Gamma Rho formed in response to the racial exclusion on and racism of their predominantly white campuses (Whaley 2009). The other four BGLOs founded at Howard University formed partly in response to the conservative political ideologies expressed by some administrators and professors, as well as to create alternative organizations that more aptly addressed their founders' desires and visions (Whaley 2009). In 1930, the National Pan-Hellenic Council (NPHC) was established as a collaborative organization to oversee the mutual interests of the "Great Eight" BGLOs. In 1963, the last of what would become the "Divine Nine" BGLO organizations, Iota Phi Theta, was founded at Morgan State University (Slade 2010).

The creation of BGLOs was not met without challenges. For example, although Kappa Alpha Psi was incorporated in the state of Indiana, they were largely unrecognized by Indiana University administrators and as such were not granted a charter on campus (Crump 1993). Accordingly, the fraternity faced obstacles to securing meeting space on campus and obtaining a fraternity house. Thus, Kappa Alpha Psi did not enjoy the same rights and privileges of white fraternal organizations (Whaley 2009). Omega Psi Phi faced similar challenges from administrators at Howard University. Administrators were slow to approve the fraternity's charter and initially stipulated changes to the fraternity's constitution that would relegate the organization to a local-only scope (Whaley 2009). However, Omega Psi Phi members were intent on creating a national organization, and eventually Howard University approved the constitution.

From the beginning, these BGLOs aimed to forge a national network of fraternity or sorority chapters. Chapters expanded to other campuses quickly, with newly chartered chapters established within the first few years of each organization's founding. Recognizing the need for chapters to be organized and uphold a cohesive platform, each organization instituted annual national conventions. The national conventions provided a space for members to discuss the organization's structure, expansion, and programs, including those dedicated to social issues.

BGLOs and their members have held pivotal roles in social movements. For example, the sorority Delta Sigma Theta was the only Black organization to participate in the Women's Suffrage March in Washington, DC, in 1913 (Giddings 2007). From World War I to World War II, BGLOs aided Black community members by filling in the economic gap caused by strained social services across the U.S. BGLOs implemented service, education, and development programs for community members during this time, as well as voiced critiques of welfare policies that they believed perpetuated racial discrimination. For example, Alpha Phi Alpha heavily criticized the New Deal in that the program was generally allocated to jobs that historically or legally barred Black participation (Weems 2013). BGLOs were also active during World War II, as sororities collaborated with charitable organizations during the war effort and delivered materials needed for the war, pushed for legislation that integrated Black women into the Navy, and supported investment in U.S. Defense Savings Bonds (Giddings 2007; Whaley 2010).

Additional political and humanitarian outreach on behalf of BGLOs took place during the Civil Rights era. The American Council on Human Rights (ACHR) was made up of six of the BGLOs and aimed to lobby Congress to pass legislation that improved rights for Blacks (Harris 2012). For example, the ACHR played a crucial role in the successful lawsuit against the Southern Railway policy of segregated seating. Additionally, many of the key figures in the Civil Rights movement were themselves members of Black Greek organizations, such as Martin Luther King, Jr. (Alpha Phi Alpha), Jesse Jackson (Omega Psi Phi), and Rosa Parks (Alpha Kappa Alpha).

Contemporary BGLOs

Many institutions of higher education have both BGLOs and historically white Greek organizations. Members of all Greek-letter organizations are likely to be leaders on campus, volunteers in the local community, and have successful academic performances. On most college campuses, Greek-letter organizations are segregated by race and overseen by different councils. Whereas the NPHC oversees BGLOs, predominantly white organizations are governed by the Inter-Fraternity Council (IFC) or the National Panhellenic Conference. People of color who join predominantly white Greek-letter organizations report being subjected to racially charged jokes or stereotypes from other members, as well as feeling isolated or disconnected from the organization as a whole (Hughey 2010). BGLOs are often considered an alternative, wherein members can receive the same networking and social opportunities, without the racial costs.

Although there are other BGLOs at campuses across the country, there are only nine that are officially recognized. These are commonly referred to as "The Divine Nine," and currently consist of four sororities (Alpha Kappa Alpha, Delta Sigma Theta, Zeta Phi Beta, and Sigma Gamma Rho) and five fraternities (Alpha Phi Alpha, Kappa Alpha Psi, Omega Psi Phi, Phi Beta Sigma, and Iota Phi Theta). BGLOs comprise undergraduate and graduate chapters as well as a national body. While most members join through chapters at their undergraduate colleges, some members join through a graduate chapter. In order to join BGLOs, the organizations invite members through a selective recruitment process that includes pledging and sometimes hazing.

Pledging is a practice of initiation for new members of BGLOs, and is seen as a way for current members to evaluate their new recruits and to decide if they should be admitted to the organization. The pledge process for BGLOs has roots in European educational institutions, which then took hold in universities in the United States (Kimbrough 2003). Shortly after the founding of BGLOs, official pledge clubs associated with each organization were instituted (Parks and Brown 2005). Pledge activities varied from school to school and evolved throughout the years. Some activities included service projects, demonstrating scholarship, and competing in athletic events against other organizations' pledges. Members of a pledge class were often required to wear matching attire and carry, protecting at all costs, insignia significant to their organization.

Pledging facilitates bonding and feelings of belonging among pledge class members and between pledges and older members. Through the pledge process, pledges face and overcome adversity together, learn about one another, and take responsibility for each other. Pledges also learn to problem solve and think creatively. By overcoming adversity in the pledge process, pledges' self-esteem and self-confidence are bolstered. The pledge process also instills feelings of pride, respect, and responsibility for and accountability to their organization. Through the shared experience of pledging, pledges not only create connections to their pledge class members and chapter members but also to organization members more broadly. BGLOs have also set themselves apart from other Greek organizations through cultural practices, such as stepping (choreographed dances), branding (marking skin with a metal iron), and calls (loud vocals). These cultural practices, symbols, and images can aid in constructing both individual and group identities for BGLOs.

This pledging process can turn into hazing if recruits are required to participate in difficult, painful, or humiliating rituals in order to gain membership. In response to an increase in negative and high-profile consequences from hazing practices, some have debated if Black fraternities and sororities should be abolished or pause membership intake (Kimbrough 2005). In acknowledgment of this controversy, the BGLO leadership has denounced hazing. However, the process still continues underground in many organizations (Foster 2008). This is in part due to the culture around pledging in BGLOs, wherein members who undergo a hazing process are construed as more genuine or authentic members than those who forgo the practice.

Black fraternities and sororities often differ significantly from their white Greek counterpoints in key ways. The organizations often receive different institutional treatment on the same campuses. Whereas white Greek organizations are more likely to have houses on campus, Black organizations often have not had the institutional support or legacy of having a house on campus, making it difficult to have influence or power within certain institutional realms (Ray and Rosow 2010). In general, white fraternities and sororities are part of a social and partying culture on campuses (Armstrong and Hamilton 2015). Therefore, individuals in white fraternities and sororities report viewing their membership as an opportunity to participate in the social life of the campus, and develop both friendships and romantic relationships (Berkowitz and Padavic 1999; Strayhorn and McCall 2011). Additionally, people of color who pledge white Greek organizations often report negative interactions with their white brothers and sisters around race, or feeling tokenized as one of the only members of color in their organization (Hughey 2010).

On the other hand, Black fraternities and sororities provide their members with a bevy of professional development skills. For example, members of BGLOs view their membership as a way to gain the skills needed to advance in their careers by being networked into a community of successful Black individuals (Hernandez and Arnold 2011). Additionally, as BGLOs engage in more community service activities as an organization than their white counterparts do, these community service opportunities provide BGLO members numerous opportunities to develop leadership skills and to serve in organizing positions (Kimbrough 1995). Importantly, BGLOs provide a space where Black students are afforded the ability to assume leadership roles where they feel assured that their opinion will not be discounted because of their race, as opposed to other clubs or organizations on predominantly white campuses (Greyerbiehl and Mitchell 2014). Finally, BGLO membership is tied to increased participation in college classes (Harper 2008).

Aside from allowing members to gain skills to advance their professional lives, Black fraternities and sororities also act to provide opportunities for personal development to their members. Black Greek members at predominantly white campuses report that their organizations serve in helping them connect to a Black community and provide a refuge from racism and discrimination on campus (Greyerbiehl and Mitchell 2014). However, the affirmative effect of BGLO membership on racial identity is not just limited to Black members on predominantly white campuses. In general, members report that BGLO membership positively influenced and shaped their racial identities and helped them feel connected to Black culture, history, and tradition (Harper 2008; Harper and Harris 2006; Greyerbiehl and Mitchell 2014). Moreover, as gendered organizations, Black fraternities and sororities aid in strengthening members' gender identities.

It is important to note that Greek-letter organizations also range beyond the Black and white binary. For example, Latino Greek-letter organizations developed in the late 1800s to provide intellectual and cultural homes for Latino students at predominantly white universities (Munoz and Guardia 2009). These underground and unofficial organizations eventually became crystallized in the form of fraternities and sororities. Similarly, Asian American fraternities and sororities were founded to provide some protection for students from racism, segregation, and discrimination that they were experiencing at predominantly white schools (Chen 2009). Recently, Native American fraternities and sororities have been established to provide support to students, as well as aid in engaging in traditions and education about Native American history (Kelly 2009). Additionally, multicultural fraternities and sororities often provide a chance for members to build cross-racial ties and foster an environment that centers on racial or social justice programming. However, these other options to white Greek-letter organizations are less numerous and robust than the BGLO system, positioning BGLOs as often the only alternative on campus to historically white Greek life.

Platforms for Racial Uplift and Activism: Then and Now

The cornerstones of BGLOs are racial justice activism and community uplift, which are evidenced through their national programs. While programs reflect the distinct focus and approach towards racial uplift of each individual organization, there are some specific issues commonly addressed by most BGLOs, such as voter registration, encouraging entrepreneurship, and educational initiatives. BGLO programming reflects central components necessary to Black individuals' full social and political citizenship in the areas of politics, economics, and education.

For example, Alpha Phi Alpha Fraternity, Incorporated's voter registration and education program, formally established in 1930, seeks to ensure Black citizens' understanding of and access to their voting rights. Though Blacks had the right to vote at the time when the program was initiated, they were prohibited from enacting that right by poll taxes, voter intimidation, and lack of education about voting. Currently restrictive voting laws continue in the form of voter ID requirements, decreases in early voting days and hours, elimination of certain voting locations, and obstacles to restoring voting rights for people with previous criminal convictions. These restrictions disproportionately affect Black and lower-income communities. As such, Alpha continues its goal to educate, empower, and register voters, coordinating its efforts under the motto "a Voteless People is a Hopeless People."

In 1924, Phi Beta Sigma Fraternity, Incorporated introduced its Bigger and Better Business program. This multifaceted program encompasses all aspects of financial literacy, entrepreneurship, and community advancement through business. Its original focus was on the establishment, maintenance, and support of Black businesses, though currently it promotes all minority-owned businesses. Through this program, Sigma desired to improve the living conditions and economic power of the Black community. One key element of the Bigger and Better Business initiative is promoting a week when Black business owners share their business knowledge and strategies for success. Chapters would often partner with Black institutions, like churches or schools, in order to provide business information to the broader Black community. As evidence of Sigma's commitment to economic independence, the fraternity opened its own credit union in 1986, which is open to fraternity members and members of Sigma's constitutionally bound sister organization, Zeta Phi Beta Sorority, Incorporated. The Bigger and Better Business program continues today as one of Sigma's key initiatives. Business acumen tailored to minority entrepreneurs is necessary as discrimination against Black business owners in obtaining credit and loans, and exploitation by predatory lenders persist (Austin 2016).

Alpha Kappa Alpha Sorority, Incorporated's oldest program of service is education. In 1914, AKA awarded its first scholarship in the amount of $10 to a Howard University student (AKA EAF n.d.). In subsequent years, AKA established a revolving loan fund for members requesting financial aid. Currently, AKA continues to provide financial educational support through its Educational Advancement Fund (EAF). Through the EAF, AKA has provided scholarships to individuals and community assistance awards, and made financial contributions to historically Black colleges and universities. In the early decades of the sorority, members, many of whom were teachers, became role models and advisors for their students. Members formally developed this role into a national organizational initiative around Vocational Guidance. In this capacity, members aided young people in qualifying for entrance in trades and other occupations. Chapters tailored their guidance and mentoring programs to fit the needs of their local communities but often included activities such as stay-in-school campaigns, occupational tours, and service bureaus. In the 1970s, AKA implemented a national reading initiative focusing on improving reading skills and comprehension among under-educated Black youth. Educational enrichment, tutoring, and mentoring activities continue to be a cornerstone of AKA programming. Accentuating the need for these interventions was the Department of Education's Office for Civil Rights report that found the present-day persistence of racial inequalities. Racial minorities are less likely to have the full range of math and science classes needed to succeed, more likely to have inexperienced teachers, and more likely to be suspended from school (U.S. Department of Education 2016).

These are but a few examples of the racial uplift and social justice focused programs initiated through BGLOs. Many of the programs originated in the early decades of BGLOs' founding as a response to the discrimination against Blacks. BGLOs continue political, economic, and educational programs, among others, because of ongoing racial disparities. Each program is enacted on the chapter level through both undergraduate and graduate chapters. To get a sense of the type of social justice work BGLOs engage in currently, a brief overview of the nationally mandated community-focused programs of each organization are listed in Table 1.1.

Non-Blacks in BGLOs

Many contemporary scholars and activists working for racial equality suggest that a crucial part of ending racism and racist practices is through multiracial contact and social movements (Kivel 1996; Pollock 2008). Gordon W. Allport's (1954) notion of "contact theory" proposes that contact between members of different racial groups promotes tolerance and a gradual decline in prejudicial attitudes and discriminatory actions. In particular, Allport suggested that cross-racial interaction that includes common goals, cooperation, and support of authorities is essential for the contact hypothesis to be successful. Increased contact between races, especially within the tight-knit and cooperative environment of a BGLO, therefore, may seem like the answer in increasingly turbulent racial times.

Although Black Greek organizations were founded as a response to policies and practices in white fraternal organizations that barred the membership of Black people, BGLOs themselves did not limit their membership only to Blacks. As early as

TABLE 1.1 BGLO Organization Information

Organization	Date founded	Place founded	Chapters	Motto	Community service programs include
Alpha Phi Alpha Fraternity	1906	Cornell University	800	"First of all, Servants of all, We shall transcend all"	A Voteless People is a Hopeless People: Voter registration and education; Go to High School, Go to College: Tutoring and mentoring program for young men; Project Alpha: Educational program for adolescent boys
Alpha Kappa Alpha Sorority	1908	Howard University	997	"By culture and by merit"	ASCEND: High school student enrichment program; AKA 1908 Playground Project: Restoration of community playgrounds; Acts of Green Program: Environmental sustainability awareness program
Kappa Alpha Psi Fraternity	1911	Indiana University	721	"Achievement in every field of human endeavor"	Kappa Alpha Psi Guide Right: Youth development program; Healthy Kappas, Healthy Communities: Health information and screenings; Kappa Kamps: Education and cultural enrichment camps for young men
Omega Psi Phi Fraternity	1911	Howard University	750	"Friendship is essential to the soul"	Achievement week: Highlights individuals who have contributed to community uplift; Talent hunt program: Cultivates, showcases, and encourages young people's involvement in the arts; College endowment fund: Contributions to historically Black colleges or universities
Delta Sigma Theta Sorority	1913	Howard University	940	"Intelligence is the torch of wisdom"	Delta Academy: Leadership development and educational enrichment program for young girls; Delta Gems: Life skills development, educational enrichment, and community service-oriented program for young women; Delta Days: Members conduct legislative visits and participate in educational sessions about best practices for effecting public policy change

Organization	Date founded	Place founded	Chapters	Motto	Community service programs include
Phi Beta Sigma Fraternity	1914	Howard University	700	"Culture for service and service for humanity"	Bigger and Better Business: Financial literacy, entrepreneurship, and community advancement through business; Project Vote: Voter registration and awareness; Living Well Brother to Brother: Health initiative geared towards health issues facing men of color
Zeta Phi Beta Sorority	1920	Howard University	850	"A community-conscious, action-oriented organization"	Elder Care Initiative: Education and preparation for elders; Stork's Nest: Through a partnership with March of Dimes, health promotion for low-income pregnant women; Zeta Premature Awareness Program: Prematurity awareness
Sigma Gamma Rho Sorority	1922	Butler University	600	"Great service, Greater progress"	Operation Big Book Bag: Supply support for schools and other educational organizations; Mwanimugimu Essay Contest: Essay contest that encourages knowledge of the historical and contemporary development of Africa; Hattie McDaniel Breast Cancer Awareness: Educational awareness and preventative health screenings for breast cancer
Iota Phi Theta Fraternity	1963	Morgan State University	300	"Building a tradition, not resting upon one"	I-S.H.I.E.L.D.: Ending abuse nationally and worldwide including human trafficking, sexual abuse, domestic abuse, elder abuse and child abuse; The I.O.T.A. Youth Alliance: Addressing the needs of Black youth in local communities; Afya Njema 360 Health Initiative: Focuses on health concerns of African American males and men of color

the 1940s, there are records of white students crossing the color-line into BGLOs (Hughey 2007). However, whites are not the only cross-race members in BGLOs. Latino and Asian students also have a limited but rich history of pledging BGLOs (Chen 2009; Hughey 2007).

For most of our respondents, BGLOs were not organizations that they were cognizant of until they arrived on their college campus. As such, interactions with members on their campus served as the main channel for their knowledge about and interest in BGLOs. About one-fourth of our respondents referenced their friendship with someone as crucial to how they learned about BGLOs and why they wanted to become a member. In these instances, their friendship preceded their BGLO membership. Respondents talked about their friends who became members or who initiated conversations about joining a BGLO. Isabella, a 40-year-old[1] Dominican sorority member, described the influence her classmates had on her decision to join a BGLO:

> There were two freshman women that I knew from a summer program I did. And I truly admired, respected, thought the world of. And they had become members of Sigma Gamma Rho. I remember running up to them like, "Oh my god, when did you do this? How did you do this?" I was so excited for them. And they said, "I know, we've been doing it all semester." I think because they were the members of this sorority, I just became very interested in that organization … I just admired these two women so much and thought the world of them and when they became members of this particular group, I thought, "Wow!"

Similarly, Roano, a 38-year-old Puerto Rican fraternity member, decided to pursue BGLO membership after his college roommate pledged:

> I think watching my roommate go through his process and have a probate and be so excited, see it as an accomplishment. He was very much accomplished in terms of his major, his academics, he was the student body president … For my roommate and I we had already established [a presence on campus] academically and socially, so I didn't feel like I needed the fraternity to continue making progress at the university. I think what excited me about joining was just a different level of commitment to the men that I respected. I made the decision at the beginning of my third year when my roommate finished his process.

Aside from having a direct connection to BGLOs through someone they knew, respondents also described how the warm reception by existing members fostered their own membership interest. Another quarter of our respondents shared stories of how their initial interactions with BGLO members served as a gateway to their eventual BGLO membership. Jessica, a 22-year-old white sorority member, explained:

> I didn't actually think that I was going to pledge anything when I came into college, 'cause, I guess the most representation I've seen is, you know, the Panhellenic, IFC, that kind of council. And that just didn't look like it was something for me. In my opinion it looked like all they really cared about was parties and that's never been me. I've always been very involved in the community, very involved with my school. It just didn't look like they were very serious or held up the standards of what they said they were. I came to [my university], I met a Delta who was here at the time and she was passing out flyers. She was very friendly, and she passed me one. And it was some of their events that were going on that semester. Me, being the open person that I am, decided to go to some of them. The more I went, the more I realized, you know, this is interesting to me. They wanted to reach out in the community and help people ... And I felt like what they were doing was making a difference in people's lives and I'd made a difference in people's lives in the past and I wanted to be part of that future.

Keung, a 30-year-old Chinese-Cambodian fraternity member, also explained how existing BGLO members' receptivity facilitated his interest.

> It came down to the people. I'd seen the other organization as well. But they were the ones that actually, kind of, more, reached out to me and were interested in the fact that I was interested in them. So they were actually the ones that kind of, made that transition of being a non-Black member, they made it feel welcoming.

In addition to personal relationships, members were drawn to BGLOs because of the character and scope of the organizations. A majority of respondents noted the commitment to community uplift, the bonds of membership, and the values of the organization as key influences on their interest. Members viewed BGLOs as a way to contribute to their communities but also to advance their own personal development. As Thomas, a 26-year-old Vietnamese-Filipino fraternity member explained, "[t]he main purpose for me was having an opportunity to be connected to people who uplifted me ... like the saying, 'Iron sharpens iron.'" Expanding on this idea more was Isabella, the Dominican sorority member, who stated:

> I thought that the women that were in the group were everything that I wanted to be. They were beautiful, dynamic, outgoing, had very good reputations, were known for being very smart, very hard working. They did community service. They always seemed to be smiling.

In addition to the personality, character, and reputation, BGLOs' considerable community engagement was an important factor in attracting our respondents. Charisse, a 23-year-old Filipina sorority member, explained:

> I also wanted to see something more beyond being into sororities that's only about college parties. I wanted more of quality. And the part that I loved the most was the lifetime membership and then it was just a respect factor that AKA has. Looking at the purpose of AKA, I kinda took my core values and then I noticed that a lot of those things were there in AKA. It was just more of the idea of being a part of something that I was going to be proud about and passionate about instead of it just being about the whole social part. How can I make an impact in society with the organizations I'm a part of?

The possibility of social impact beyond college was also what drew Bradley, a 23-year-old white fraternity member. He shared:

> I wanted to feel like I was a part of something that would carry with me throughout my life after college. I felt like I had done a lot of things that were temporary and not necessarily lasting. I wanted to make a lasting impression on my campus and do something that would make a lasting impression on my life as well.

Echoing Bradley's statement about the importance of having a lasting impact was Binh, a 29-year-old Vietnamese fraternity member, who explained his reason for membership:

> So I joined Alpha for the community that was really social justice oriented and professional. Our values aligned a lot more and I could invest in an organization that would be relationships that would carry me past graduation, meaning beyond just my chapter. And so I thought it was the best decision as far as who would push me professionally and personally, academically, of course, but personally and professionally and at the same time be committed to improving the world.

Overall, our respondents reflect previous findings on non-Black members' motivations for joining. Often, non-Black members cite that a specific individual influenced their decision to join, such as a friend or mentor who may have been a member of the particular BGLO that they pledged (Hughey 2007). Other cross-racial members may pledge BGLOs because they wish to be a part of their community service projects or networking opportunities, of which BGLOs tend to have more than their white counterparts (Hughey 2007). Finally, some members' motivations to join may come from a commitment to live racial equality or to purposefully integrate their friend group and social network (Hughey 2008).

Adding to these reasons for membership are other external factors. Some non-Blacks state that their own personal experience or familiarity with Black culture or community motivated their pledging process, with BGLO membership feeling like a natural extension of the majority-Black neighborhoods or schools that they were immersed in prior to college (Hughey 2007). Similarly, many Latino or Asian BGLO members report joining in order to find a refuge among other students of color (Hughey 2007). For example, Asian American students may join BGLOs because they view membership as a natural outgrowth of their identification with other racial minorities over whites and as a venue to further develop a non-white racial identity (Chen 2009). Particularly on campuses with little racial diversity, joining a BGLO may help provide important social and emotional outlets for otherwise isolated students of color. We turn to these membership factors in the next two chapters.

Despite crossing the color-line, evidence suggests that some non-Black members of Black fraternities and sororities still hold racist stereotypes and problematic notions of Black culture. For example, some white members of BGLOs aim to take central roles in leadership in order to act as a savior to what they see as organizations in need of resources (Hughey 2008). Additionally, some non-Black BGLO members believe that their membership is evidence that race is no longer a salient factor in the United States today (Hughey 2008).

Because Black fraternities and sororities historically have been central places of racial uplift and community for Black students, the entrance of non-Black individuals into these organizations has been controversial (Kimbrough 2003). Some worry that non-Black membership could transform BGLOs away from servicing and reflecting the Black community and remove a vital social resource from Black students (Ross 2002). Accordingly, some non-Black members report hostility from Blacks, both within and outside their organizations (Hughey 2007). However, others point out that much of the controversial reaction to non-Black BGLO members comes from within the racial group of the non-Black member, who may view cross-racial membership as antithetical or threatening to their racial identity (Hughey 2007).

Non-Blacks entering into Black organizations provide a rich case study for how people navigate and understand racial differences. On one hand, these racial boundary crossers embody the integration of races which fits into the contemporary ideology of colorblindness, while on the other hand, they may represent the takeover of spaces that historically have been central places of Black racial uplift and community. Despite the illuminating details that non-Black BGLO members can provide about racial identity and race in contemporary institutions of higher education, the research on non-Black BGLO members is limited. This is particularly true of research that investigates the experiences of non-Black BGLO members outside the pledging process and their initial motivations for joining a cross-racial organization. There is a particular need for additional research that explores the impact of non-Black membership on their lives outside and beyond college. We turn to these issues in the following chapters.

Note

1 Throughout the book, we report the age that the participants were during their interview with us, in order to provide context for their comments.

References

AKA EAF (n.d.). "History." Educational Advancement Foundation. https://akaeaf.org/history

Allport, Gordon W. 1954. *The Nature of Prejudice*. Reading, MA: Addison-Wesley.

Armstrong, Elizabeth A., and Laura T. Hamilton. 2015. *Paying for the Party: How College Maintains Inequality*. Cambridge, MA: Harvard University Press.

Austin, Algernon. 2016. *The Color of Entrepreneurship: Why the Racial Gap among Firms Costs the U.S. Billions*. Washington, DC: Center for Global Policy Studies.

Berkowitz, Alexandra and Irene Padavic. 1999. "Getting a Man or Getting Ahead: A Comparison of White and Black Sororities." *Journal of Contemporary Ethnography* 27(4):530–555.

Billingsley, Andrew. 1999. *Mighty Like A River: The Black Church and Social Reform*. New York, NY: Oxford University Press.

Butler, Anne S. 2012. "Black Fraternal and Benevolent Societies in Nineteenth-Century America." Pp. 75–100 in *African American Fraternities and Sororities: The Legacy and the Vision*, edited by T.L. Brown, G.S. Parks, and C.M. Phillips. Lexington, KY: University Press of Kentucky.

Chen, Edith Wen-Chu. 2009. "Asian Americans in Sororities and Fraternities." Pp. 83–103 in *Brothers and Sisters*, edited by C.L. Torbenson and G.S. Parks. Madison, WI: Fairleigh Dickinson University Press.

Crump, William L. 1993. *The Story of Kappa Alpha Psi: A History of the Beginnings and Development of a College Greek Letter Organization, 1911–1991*, 4th Ed. Philadelphia, PA: Kappa Alpha Psi Fraternity International Headquarters.

Du Bois, W.E.B. 1903. *The Souls of Black Folk*. Chicago: A. C. McClurg & Co.

Foster, Kevin Michael. 2008. "Black Greeks and Underground Pledging: Public Debates and Communal Concerns." *Transforming Anthropology* 16(1):3–19.

Giddings, Paula J. 2007. *In Search of Sisterhood: Delta Sigma Theta and the Challenge of the Black Sorority Movement*. New York, NY: HarperCollins.

Greyerbiehl, Lindsay, and Donald Mitchell Jr. 2014. "An Intersectional Social Capital Analysis of the Influence of Historically Black Sororities on African American Women's College Experiences at a Predominantly White Institution." *Journal of Diversity in Higher Education* 7(4):282–294.

Harper, Shaun R. 2008. "The Effects of Sorority and Fraternity Membership on Class Participation and African American Student Engagement in Predominantly White Classroom Environments." *College Student Affairs Journal* 27(1):94–115.

Harper, Shaun R., and Frank Harris. 2006. "The Role of Black Fraternities in the African American Male Undergraduate Experience." Pp. 129–153 in *African American Men in College*, edited by M.J. Cuyjet. San Francisco, CA: Jossey-Bass.

Harris, Jr., Robert L. 2012. "Lobbying Congress for Civil Rights: The American Council on Human Rights, 1948–1963." Pp. 213–231 in *African American Fraternities and Sororities: The Legacy and the Vision*, 2nd Ed., edited by T.L. Brown, G.S. Parks, and C.M. Phillips. Lexington, KY: University Press of Kentucky.

Hernandez, Marcia, and Harriett Arnold. 2011. "'The Harvest is Plentiful but the Laborers are Few': An Interdisciplinary Examination of Career Choice and African American Sororities." *Journal of African American Studies* 16(4):658–673.

Hughey, Matthew W. 2007. "Crossing the Sands, Crossing the Color Line: Non-Black Members of Black Greek Letter Organizations." *Journal of African American Studies* 11(1):55–75.

Hughey, Matthew W. 2008. "'I Did it for the Brotherhood': NonBlack Members in Black Greek-Letter Organizations." Pp. 313–343 in *Black Greek-Letter Organizations in the 21st Century*, edited by G.S. Parks. Lexington, KY: University Press of Kentucky.

Hughey, Matthew W. 2010. "A Paradox of Participation: Nonwhites in White Sororities and Fraternities." *Social Problems* 57(4):653–679.

Hughey, Matthew W. (Ed.) 2013. *Race and Ethnicity in Secret and Exclusive Social Orders: Blood and Shadow.* New York, NY: Taylor & Francis.

Kelly, Linda. 2009. "Preserving and Creating Traditions: A Native American Emergence in Greek Organizations." Pp. 133–156 in *Brothers and Sisters*, edited by C.L. Torbenson and G.S. Parks. Madison, WI: Fairleigh Dickinson University Press.

Kimbrough, Walter M. 1995. "Self-Assessment, Participation, and Value of Leadership Skills, Activities, and Experiences for Black Students Relative to their Membership in Historically Black Fraternities and Sororities." *The Journal of Negro Education* 64(1):63–74.

Kimbrough, Walter M. 2003. *Black Greek 101: The Culture, Customs, and Challenges of Black Fraternities and Sororities.* Madison, WI: Farleigh Dickinson University Press.

Kimbrough, Walter M. 2005. "Should Black Fraternities and Sororities Abolish Under-graduate Chapters?" *About Campus* 10:27–29.

Kivel, Paul. 1996. *Uprooting Racism: How White People Can Work for Racial Justice.* New York, NY: New Society Publishers.

Lincoln, C. Eric, and Lawrence H. Mamiya. 1990. *The Black Church in the African American Experience.* Durham, NC: Duke University Press.

Moore, Jacqueline M. 1999. *Leading the Race: The Transformation of the Black Elite in the Nation's Capital: 1880–1920.* Charlottesville, VA: The University Press of Virginia.

Munoz, Susana M., and Juan R. Guardia. 2009. "Latino/a Fraternities and Sororities." Pp. 103–132 in *Brothers and Sisters*, edited by C.L. Torbenson and G.S. Parks. Madison, WI: Fairleigh Dickinson University Press.

Parks, Gregory S., and Tamara L. Brown. 2005. "'In the Fell Clutch of Circumstance': Pledging and the Black Greek Experience." Pp. 437–464 in *African American Fraternities and Sororities: The Legacy and the Vision*, edited by T.L. Brown, G.S. Parks, and C.M. Phillips. Lexington, KY: University Press of Kentucky.

Pollock, Mica. 2008. *Everyday Anti Racism: Getting Real About Race in School.* New York, NY: The New Press.

Ray, Rashawn, and Jason A. Rosow. 2010. "Getting Off and Getting Intimate: How Normative Institutional Arrangements Structure Black and White Fraternity Men's Approaches Toward Women." *Men and Masculinities* 12(5):523–546.

Ross, Lawrence C. 2002. *The Divine Nine: The History of African American Fraternities and Sororities.* New York, NY: Dafina Books.

Ross, Rosetta E. 2003. *Witnessing and Testifying: Black Women, Religion, and Civil Rights.* Minneapolis, MN: Augsburg Fortress.

Skocpol, Theda, Ariane Liazos and Marshall Ganz. 2006. *What a Mighty Power We Can Be: African American Fraternal Groups and the Struggle for Racial Equality*. Princeton, NJ: Princeton University Press.

Slade, John D. 2010. *Iota Phi Theta: The Founding and Ascendancy: A Founder's Perspective*. San Francisco, CA: Iota Icon Publishing.

Strayhorn, Terrell L. and Fred C. McCall. 2011. "Black Greek-Letter Organizations at Predominantly White Institutions and Historically Black Colleges and Universities." Pp. 277–292 in *Black Greek-Letter Organizations 2.0: New Directions in the Study of African American Fraternities*, edited by M.W. Hughey and G.S. Parks. Jackson, MI: University Press of Mississippi.

U.S. Department of Education. 2016. *2013–2014 Civil Rights Data Collection: A First Look*. Washington, DC: U.S. Department of Education, Office of Civil Rights.

Warnock, Raphael G. 2014. *The Divided Mind of the Black Church: Theology, Piety, and Public Witness*. New York, NY: New York University Press.

Weems, Jr., Robert E. 2013. "Alpha Phi Alpha, the Fight for Civil Rights and the Shaping of Public Policy." Pp. 233–262 in *Alpha Phi Alpha: A Legacy of Greatness, the Demands of Transcendence*, edited by G.S. Parks and S.M. Bradley. Lexington, KY: University Press of Kentucky.

Wesley, Charles H. 1995. *The History of Alpha Phi Alpha: A Development in College Life*. Baltimore, MD: The Foundation Publishers.

Whaley, Deborah Elizabeth. 2009. "Links, Legacies, and Letters: A Cultural History of Black Greek-Letter Organizations." Pp. 46–82 in *Brothers and Sisters*, edited by C.L. Torbenson and G.S. Parks. Madison, WI: Fairleigh Dickinson University Press.

Whaley, Deborah Elizabeth. 2010. *Disciplining Women: Alpha Kappa Alpha, Black Counterpublics, and the Cultural Politics of Black Sororities*. Albany, NY: State University of New York Press.

2

"I'M NOT TRYING TO BE YOU"

Identity and Boundary Work

> But I didn't join this because I think I'm something other than who I am. I'm not trying to be you. I'm white. I'm from [the Midwest]. I know exactly who I am.
>
> *Kelly, 42-year-old white sorority member*

When identifying with and pledging a Black Greek-letter Organization (BGLO), non-Black members must confront the contemporary color-line in a very direct way. As we discussed briefly in Chapter 1, their motivations to enter into a Black organization vary, from interest in the mission, desire to perform community service projects, and already established bonds with a BGLO member. By declaring their association across racial boundaries, these members of Black fraternities and sororities often experience a reconstitution of how they conceive of their own racial identities, as well as how they understand and conceptualize race within the world around them.

The entrance of non-Black members into the specifically racialized organizations of Black Greek life is influenced by both symbolic and social boundaries. Symbolic boundaries are the divisions between objects, people, and practices that operate as a "system of rules that guide interaction by affecting who comes together to engage in what social act" (Lamont and Fournier 1992:12). Symbolic boundaries, therefore, classify objects, define hierarchy, and justify the distribution of resources and meanings across a particular setting. Moreover, symbolic boundaries are integral to identity because they help to differentiate "oneself from others by drawing on criteria such as common traits and experiences as well as a sense of shared belonging" (Small et al. 2010:18).

Therefore, non-Black BGLO members, like Kelly, utilize symbolic boundaries, such as emphasizing her authentic white identity, to understand and conceptualize themselves in relation to the organization as a whole. Social boundaries, on the other hand, reflect how social differences manifest in the unequal distribution of resources. Although BGLOs can be understood as resource-rich organizations that distribute material resources to traditionally marginalized and under-networked Black members, we argue that symbolic resources, such as racial identities and belonging are also being accomplished in these organizations via the relationships between members. These symbolic identities are especially pronounced with non-Black members, who must navigate the differences between their own racial background and that of their organization.

Educational settings have long served as a site for drawing and redrawing racial lines and blurring symbolic boundaries. Previous research has addressed the relationship between symbolic boundaries and ethnic and racial divisions in educational settings, finding that multiethnic school environments can both enhance and aid in diffusing racial boundaries (Warikoo 2010). In particular, the structure of the educational environment, including size, history of efforts to improve race relations, and the amount of time given for social interaction seem to encourage diffuse boundaries across racial lines. Given these characteristics, it would seem that the close-knit, racial justice-oriented social setting of BGLOs would provide an ideal environment for transgressing boundaries based on racial differences.

In this chapter, we highlight how non-Black BGLO members go about the ongoing accomplishment of reforming their identities and finding belonging in these majority-Black networks and communities. We first describe how our respondents conceptualized and strategized crossing the color-line via their membership into Black fraternities and sororities. After deciding to enter into Black organizations, many non-Black members reported that their understandings of race, racism, and discrimination were heightened. This occurred via both the personal connections that they developed within their BGLOs, as well as through a new view on the institutional constraints that were leveled at their organization. Many respondents also had their racial identities strengthened, either by feeling like the odd non-Black person out in their group of friends or discovering their own racial identity in contrast and comparison to Blackness. The impact of their organizational membership on their identities also reflected how they viewed and understood their gender identities, as well as the connection between race and gender, which we explore at the end of the chapter.

"It Says 'Servants of All'": Strategies for Crossing the Color-Line

For many of our respondents, BGLOs were not organizations that they were familiar with until they arrived on their college campus. Because of this lack of awareness, the initial steps for non-Blacks to join a traditionally Black Greek-letter organization were major barriers to racial boundary transgression. Crossing is a term utilized in BGLOs to indicate that a new member has been fully initiated into the fraternity or sorority. However, non-Black individuals interested in BGLOs must also grapple with how to cross the color-line and must conceptualize their participation in a resoundingly Black space.

Our non-Black BGLO respondents described distinct strategies in approaching an organization that resided across the color-line. These approaches varied widely in terms of how salient respondents felt that their non-Black identity was within the organization and what they conceptualized as the goal of their racial boundary crossing. Previous research has also documented how non-Black BGLO members approach and understand their membership within a Black organization. Sociologist Matthew W. Hughey (2008) reported four types of white BGLO members, including those who entered with a goal of improving race relations but who also take over leadership positions, indicative of a type of paternalism; those who aim for a post-racial society via their membership; those who chase after what they view as a more authentic racial identity through their membership in a Black organization; and those who wish for racial diversity and see Black-controlled and -dominated BGLOs as an obstacle to this goal.

Our participants' experiences mirror this previous research in some ways, but also add nuanced contours. We document four ways that respondents expressed their approaches to joining and participating in a BGLO as a non-Black member: colorblind crossing, in which race was seen as unimportant or as a distasteful reason for joining; careful crossing, in which respondents recognized that they were crossing a color-line and wished to proceed cautiously; challenging by crossing, wherein respondents characterized their membership as an intentional desire to break down racial barriers; and collective crossing, wherein respondents of color felt categorized within a larger Black racial category and joined as a response to this classification. We explore the details of these approaches to crossing the color-line below.

Colorblind Crossing

One of the major barriers to joining a BGLO for non-Black members was around the salience of race on their college campus. For some respondents, however, the decision to join a BGLO was not seen as crossing a racial barrier. These respondents drew upon ideas of colorblindness to explain their BGLO membership, such as that they do not "see race" or that they "don't judge people by their skin color." Colorblindness, therefore, allows individuals to imagine that race has no impact on the opportunities afforded to individuals or their life outcomes (Gallagher 2003). Previous research has shown that colorblindness plays a role in how some non-Black individuals enter into BGLOs, with them considering their membership evidence of the existence of in a post-racial society (Hughey 2008).

For our respondents who conceptualized their membership through colorblind crossing, BGLOs, though historically Black, were reimagined as colorblind spaces where social bonding and common goals trumped race. It is also notable to mention that this strategy was particular to BGLO members who identified as white or white multiracial. For example, in a conversation with Amber, a 31-year-old white sorority member, Wendy asked her if race impacted her decision to join her sorority at a large public university. Amber responded by stating:

You know it really didn't. I think, I felt, the thing about me is I pretty much, I hang out with anyone … So my decision to join [my BGLO] was purely based on the principles and the people. It's just kind of, I liked the organization, so I joined it.

For Amber, her membership was one of fit based solely on shared principles and personality. Race was neither a motivation nor a barrier to pledging. Instead, she simply "liked the organization, so [she] joined it." Jessica, a 22-year-old white sorority member, also did not see her experience joining a BGLO as highlighting race or racial differences. She explained, "I guess [I see myself first as a] member of my sorority because it doesn't involve in my mind anything that necessarily has to do with race. I can say I'm a member of [my BGLO] and I don't have to tell people, 'Oh, I'm white. Or you're Black or you're a Mexican or you're Asian.' It just means that I'm a person."

Although her sorority at her private university was founded on principles of racial uplift and has a strong history of racial justice advocacy, Jessica states that the organization "doesn't involve in [her] mind anything that necessarily has to do with race." In order to make sense of this paradox, Jessica expresses a colorblind logic of "I'm a person" in order to de-racialize her own racial identity, as well as the racial identity of her BGLO. Carley, a 23-year-old white-Egyptian sorority member, expresses a similar sentiment: "Because I see [my BGLO] as, like, an organization that holds itself to a higher standard. Not, I see it as something that separates itself from other people. I don't see that it has really anything to do with race. Yes, we do have a primary focus on the Black community."

Carley's response highlights a paradox. On one hand, like Jessica, Carley characterizes her BGLO's principles as the defining characteristic, as opposed to the organization as primarily organized around race and racial issues. However, on the other hand, she identifies that race, in fact, does play an important role in the programming of the organization. Carley's paradox showcases the mental gymnastics that members of organizations that are explicitly race-based must achieve in order to claim that the organization is actually race-neutral.

Some respondents initially approached BGLOs as racialized organizations, but changed their minds after joining and participating in them. For example, Stacey, a 30-year-old white sorority member, shared how she became comfortable in joining a BGLO at her public university although she initially perceived her race to be a barrier to membership:

Well, interestingly enough, when I first met the ladies of my organization … I went up to them and asked them if I could even do community service with them because I knew that they were a traditionally and historically African American organization … They were like, "You can come and do whatever you want with us" and it made me feel very welcomed with them.

> I think my own identity, at first, kinda stopped me from being interested in an organization that was lifelong and dedicated to community service but after really getting to know the women as well as the people on my campus, it made it very apparent that my race didn't mean a whole lot.

In her first interactions with her sorority, Stacey acknowledged the symbolic boundary of race for participation in BGLOs. However, once she interacted with sorority members, she decided "race didn't mean a whole lot." While Stacey initially approached the organization as inherently racialized, by the end of her excerpt we see her de-racializing the organization as a race-neutral organization "that was lifelong and dedicated to community service."

Similarly, Chris, a 22-year-old white fraternity member, described how joining a BGLO at his public university aided in effectively diluting his white racial identity and his understanding of how race impacted society, saying:

> I think when I was in high school and everything, my white identity was probably stronger. When I got to college [and joined my fraternity] and I got to see there were so many different, so many different races and so many different background, cultures, religions, everything, I think that it became more of a, that we're all together. It's not necessarily, "Oh, I'm white. This my identity" but it just, I think it became more of "We're all people."

Although colorblind statements that deemphasize the importance of race in society may initially appear progressive or transformative, they effectively work in denying the very real opportunities and outcomes that are structured by race in society, such as racial job discrimination or mass incarceration of people of color. However, especially for white individuals like these respondents, thinking that race is no longer a meaningful categorization in society may be particularly comforting and a way to assuage any guilt that comes from understanding the racial privileges that whites experience throughout society. This perspective mirrors previous research that has documented that white individuals often turn to ideals of colorblindness, such as emphasizing humanity instead of racial categories, in order to deal with their discomfort around race and racial differences (Bonilla-Silva 2010).

These colorblind responses from the participants reveal the paradox of their meritocratic position. These white BGLO members expressed that race was not a motivating factor, concern, or issue in pledging or participating in a Greek fraternal organization; however, they acknowledge the centrality of race whether in interactions with other members, their hesitations in joining, and the specific goals, histories and missions of the BGLOs. Respondents emphasized their own shared values and ideals with their organization as evidence that racial differences were unimportant and meaningless.

Careful Crossing

Whereas colorblind crossers de-emphasized the role of race in their fraternal associations, other respondents expressed awareness that BGLO membership would cause them to cross a salient social and racial boundary. In order to remedy this, respondents took precautions to ensure that they would be truly welcomed within their BGLO. Often, non-Black members used the indicator of other non-Black members within their organization in order to cautiously navigate their bridging across racial lines.

It was important to careful crossers that they were not the only ones to traverse the color-line in their particular organization or chapter. Many respondents described historical examples of cross-racial membership as an illustration of a tradition of inclusion within their BGLO. For example, Sofia, a 27-year-old Latina and white sorority member, called upon the history of color-line crossing within her particular organization, saying:

> First of all, if people really knew our history, you know, one of my sorors, her name is Joan Trumpauer (Mulholland), she crossed at Tougaloo in 1964. She was the first white student at Tougaloo. She's a freedom rider. So it's just like, I'm not the first and I won't be the last.

For Sofia, it was important that there was a well-established history of non-Black members within her organization as this signaled to her that her organization would be open to her membership. Even if most people are unfamiliar with Joan Trumpauer Mulholland and her membership in a BGLO, many have seen her without knowing it. In the pictures of the Jackson, Mississippi Woolworth sit-in on May 28, 1963, Joan is the white young woman sitting at the counter between Lois Chaffee, a white man, and Anne Moody, a Black young woman. Prior to the 1963 sit-in, Joan, then 19 years old, joined the 1961 Mississippi Freedom Ride. She and other riders were jailed for two months on death row at the Parchman Penitentiary in Mississippi. After her release from jail, Joan became the first white student at Tougaloo College in Jackson, Mississippi.

Respondents also cited more localized and contemporary examples of previous color-line crossers as inspiring or normalizing their own cross-racial membership. Bradley, a 23-year-old white fraternity member, explained:

> I had spoken to some of the members of the chapter before I joined, and you know, asked them, "How common is this? … Am I going to be like *the one guy* at all the events?" And they told me that like, most of them had at least met a white brother, or a brother that was not Black.

The possibility of being put into a situation where Bradley might be "the one [white] guy" at all of his fraternity events made him anxious. It is interesting to note that this experience of being a token member of a racial group is not foreign to most people of color, especially within the context of higher education, where many people of color have experiences of being among a sea of white individuals. However, this possibility gave Bradley pause until his brothers were able to assure him that he would not be the only one. For Osita, a 33-year-old Puerto Rican sorority member, knowing others who had crossed before her also helped. She stated: "There was a particular individual who was a graduate student when I was in undergrad, who was actually a Latina female as well. She played a large role in seeing her as a Latina female and seeing her in an NPHC [National Pan-Hellenic Council] organization."

Even open mission statements could convey the message that non-Black members would be accepted. Chris, the white fraternity member, explained:

> When I was researching, one thing that really caught me was the fact that they stress inclusion rather than exclusion, which really went with my whole outlook on life and how I view everybody. I definitely noticed that they like to include diversity and that when they were founded, they were founded on the idea of inclusion rather than exclusion.

Discussions of the original intent behind founding BGLOs were commonly expressed among our participants as indicators that it would be safe to cross the color-line into a Black Greek organization. Roano, a 38-year-old Puerto Rican fraternity member, explained how the mission statement of his fraternity led him to advocate for cross-racial inclusion in his chapter at a public university: "I think my presence as a Latino male has been a benefit to the fraternity. I think because I continue to push back on concepts of 'We will only work for the Black community' versus following our motto, which is 'First of all, servants of all.' It doesn't say service of all Blacks, it says servants of all."

Kelly, the white sorority member, explained how important the mission statement was to her feeling that she could have a space in her membership despite her race:

> [Non-Black membership] is rare and I understand that but if we all understand our history, we all can point to times when our organizations saw the need to not be exclusively Black. You know, we made a decision at a national convention in 1954 that we're not going to discriminate by basis of race or ethnicity. I know we're, you know, a sisterhood of Black college-educated women but I can contribute to the cause and the focus of what this organization is about also.

These respondents appreciated that their organizations had clear mission statements that did not exclude non-Black members, but rather made space for them to establish themselves as a non-Black member who aimed still to contribute to their organizations' focuses on racial inclusion and equality. For the careful crossers, it was imperative that they had a historical reference for validating their membership, as well as giving them a signal that crossing would be acceptable or welcome. Their knowledge of previous non-Black members served as a source of legitimacy. These respondents acknowledged the racial symbolic boundary that continued to characterize BGLOs as for Black members only, yet drew upon well-known instances of boundary crossing to make sense of their own desire for membership. Through this discursive move, respondents not only registered the symbolic boundary within BGLOs but also within the contours of their own racial group. Therefore, their color-line crossing is both *into* BGLO membership and *out of* the lines of their own racial group.

Challenging by Crossing

In contrast to colorblind crossers who disavowed the importance of the color-line within their BGLO membership and careful crossers who were aware of the color-line and timidly crossed it, we also talked to non-Black BGLO members who consciously and confidently crossed the color-line into their BGLO. These respondents recognized the color-line and described their membership as being motivated by an intentional desire to break down racial barriers. For these members, joining a BGLO was not solely a pathway towards personal connec-tions or shared social interests, but instead represented a step towards a larger vision of racial equality and desegregation. This strategy was used predominantly by white respondents who believed that the white/non-white racial divide must be challenged by the integration of whiteness into spaces of color.

For example, Michael, a 22-year-old white fraternity member, explained, "I had gone to only Black schools my entire life. That was kinda a big part of who I was, this person who wanted to break barriers that kind of held us, you know, apart." Whereas Michael had not chosen his pre-college educational settings, being a white student at mostly Black schools became "a part of who [he] was." Once he arrived at college, Michael envisioned joining a BGLO as a white man as part of a larger mission to break down racial barriers between people.

Similarly, Adam, a 39-year-old white fraternity member, described his membership:

> It was the bigger picture that of just breaking down racial barriers. I was like, where I am currently at that time, you know, people from the Black side of the cafeteria were not gonna cross over to the white side of the cafeteria. But my friends were there so that's where I was gonna go. So it was kind of like a larger statement of, you know, there is definitely a divide here and I don't want to be on that side. I want to be on the right side, I guess, for me is what it felt like.

Both Adam and Michael described their BGLO membership as an intentional decision linked to purposely challenging and bridging racial divides. As opposed to the colorblind reasoning described earlier, these participants recognized racial segregation as a true social problem. Justin, a 22-year-old white fraternity member, characterized his membership in a more utilitarian manner:

> So, it started when one of my line brothers sent me an email and was like, "Hey, look. This organization wants to charter here at [my university]. You know, you're the type of person that loves taking on challenges and I feel like you would be interested in this." I kinda realized that you know this was an opportunity for me to expand, you know, everything I knew about Greek life and about culture. I love being the white guy in the Black frat and how society views that.

Justin constructed his membership as a chance to stand out and challenge racial assumptions about who should or should not pledge a Black fraternity. For Justin, BGLO membership was conceived of as a site in which to construct his identity as someone who does not easily fit into normative social groups or organizations.

These participants' comments underscore a view of organizations and associations of color as being equivalent to other types of racial segregation, and moreover, as something that needed to be challenged by whites entering into these spaces of color. This reasoning reflects previous research that has found that some non-Black members entered with a goal of improving race relations by purposefully diversifying their organization (Hughey 2008). Often, this strategy is particular to white individuals who assume that their whiteness will be an automatic benefit to the organization, in terms of the leadership skills, the social networks, or material resources that they bring.

This viewpoint ignores the role of white racism in the initial reasons for the founding of BGLOs and Black-centric social spaces. Additionally, it discounts the possible negative impacts of whites entering into spaces that still provide social and political inclusion for marginalized members of society. In contrast to careful crossers whose comments expressed some hesitancy for BGLO membership because of the acknowledgement of crossing into Blackness, and potentially experiencing social or racial exclusion, individuals who used challenging by crossing viewed their whiteness as a justification and obligation for their crossing. In doing so, they viewed BGLOs as institutions that could be benefited or enhanced by their entrance as a white individual.

Commonality Crossing

Challenging by crossing was utilized mainly by white respondents who believed that the white/non-white racial divide must be challenged by the integration of whiteness into spaces of color. In contrast, for many of our Latino and Asian respondents, their membership was an aim to form bonds with other students of color due to their racialized experiences on their college campus. For most of these respondents, a palpable color-line loomed large on their college campuses, often grouping white students against those categorized by others as Black. This color-line was noticeable because of the overall small numbers of students of color on many of these college campuses, as well as the different priorities and experiences that white students had as compared to students of color.

Although these respondents identified neither as Black nor white, due to the overall small population of students of color on their particular campus, these participants reported feeling forced by others into the category of "Black." Respondents described the dichotomization of the 'Black' or 'white' categories on their campuses as having an important role in social options and outlets. The lack of social opportunities and organizations around other identities of color played an important part in Latino and Asian participants' motivations to traverse the color-line and join a historically Black organization. Khashifa, a 35-year-old Pakistani sorority member, explained this logic:

> The environment was very divided. It was … you were either white or you were Black. You were not anything in between … I just kinda felt like an outcast. And so, when I, you know, started to make friends at the University and started to meet people. I ended up meeting more minorities and I learned more about the African American community on campus, and that's where I felt comfortable. And through that I learned about Greek life.

For Khashifa, the lack of students that fell outside of the Black/white racial binary on her private university's campus led her to feel isolated and alone. However, once she realized her commonalities with Black students on campus, she found a social group where she began to feel comfortable. It was through this experience that Black Greek life felt like a natural fit. Similarly, Todd, a 20-year-old Mexican-Japanese fraternity member, explained how his private university's racial climate influenced his decision to join a BGLO:

> Well, I actually hadn't planned on joining [a fraternity] when I got into college. I didn't really know about them. But once I was at [college] which is a white predominantly institution, I noticed a lot of the other students were in Greek-letter organizations. The more I researched the Greek organizations we had on campus, the, the white fraternities, they didn't really fit me. In fact, me being a minority myself, but not Black, but a minority still, I didn't really fit in with the white students on campus, and the Black community actually accepted me more.

While Todd did not identify as Black, he realized that he "didn't really fit in with the white students on campus." Through his identification as a person of color, he found commonalities with the Black community and felt that joining a BGLO made more sense for his racial identity than joining a predominantly white fraternity.

For some respondents, their prior experiences and comfort around the Black community led them to feel commonalities that drew them to pledge BGLOs. For example, Binh, a 29-year-old Vietnamese fraternity member, shared:

> I went to a predominantly African American high school and transitioned to a predominantly white institution. It is really jarring as far as the cultural differences, which kind of pushed me back into the community that supported me through my high school and then continued to support me in college. So most of my friends ended up being Black just 'cause, that's kinda how I grew up anyways, and it was just easier for me to congregate towards that.

For Binh, joining a BGLO was a response to a stark racial divide on his small private college campus that felt "really jarring." Due to his previous experience in a predominantly Black high school, Binh once again sought out the Black community in order to find support and social outlets.

Some of the reasons why these respondents chose to pledge a BGLO were because they felt that the programming and mission of the organization better reflected their interests as students of color than their white counterparts. Many respondents explained that the social justice and community service orientation of BGLOs drew them across the color-line, as they felt a common goal between themselves and the Black members. For example, Osita, the Puerto Rican sorority member, highlighted the difference between her BGLO and the white sororities that she considered: "I had a vibe and feeling early on that [white] sororities were not a best fit for me. That wasn't something that I felt aligned with who I was and my cultural identity." Alessandra, a 44-year-old Guatemalan sorority member, explicitly drew a connection between Latino and Black communities' fight for racial justice, stating:

> I was always of the premise and understanding that Black and Brown organizations fight for equity. We fight for and stand up for situations that are anti-oppression that are anti-racist and so my voice lended to this organization would be, anything that we could do within our organization to promote the programs of education, around educating Black women, would only help to support also educating brown women, also bringing out some of the causes that effect Black and brown society. So for me it was, I was, I think I was very much informed and educated around the fact that our causes were not exact but somewhat similar and in joining this organization I would also be assisting each other because if we lift one up we kind of lift both up.

Similarly, Sri, a 37-year-old Bangladeshi fraternity member, explained that he felt that BGLOs could better relate to what he felt were important issues and topics as a Muslim man, saying:

> I am Muslim and that was a huge, huge decision why I wanted to join this organization 'cause just the compassion and the level of brotherhood that I saw in this fraternity. It's the most amazing thing when you come from the other side of the world and you're able to see life in the same lens as someone in this organization.

On college campuses that centered racial experiences through a Black/white binary, Latino and Asian respondents constructed their racial identity through this lens, leading them to identify with Blackness and spurring them to join BGLOs. This was partly because some non-Black BGLO members of color felt that Black students could better relate to their experiences on their college campuses, but also because they felt that Black students and BGLOs shared their interest in community service and programming about racial equality more so than white students and white fraternal organizations. In this way, these students demonstrate the idea of a type of linked fate (Dawson 1995) between students of color from different racial backgrounds on the college campus.

"I Really Didn't Understand Racism Until I Had to See it from That Point of View": Identifying Racism

Regardless of their strategies for entering and participating in BGLOs, the majority of the non-Black BGLO members we talked to found their experiences within their respective organizations as eye-opening. For some of these members, they had not spent a significant amount of time within a majority-Black community until they joined their Greek organization. Suddenly, they found themselves in organizations not only populated almost entirely by Black individuals, but also that were founded on notions of building a strong Black community. Because of this, conversations about race in general, and Blackness in particular, were fairly common among our respondents and other members of their Greek organizations.

Understanding Through Personal Connections

This exposure to a different racial experience from their own allowed these BGLO members to reflect upon the role of race and discrimination in society. It also provided respondents with tools to identify racism, especially for individuals who felt that they had not experienced discrimination prior to their entrance into their fraternity or sorority. This was particularly pronounced for white BGLO members, many of whom may have downplayed the salience of race even upon their entrance into their historically Black organization.

For example, Justin, the white fraternity member, found that his membership changed how he thought about and understood race. He explained that the initial intake and pledging process of his BGLO provided him with an opportunity to think about implicit racial bias for the first time. He said:

> I'm definitely more culturally aware. I thought going into it, I was super culturally aware and that I knew so much, having taken so many sociology classes and growing up in a very liberal city. But I have, you know, gotten a first-hand like rude awakening in terms of how ignorant I really was.

For Justin, even though he was seeking out an organization across the color-line and felt that he was very "culturally aware," it was not until he was immersed in the process of actually joining that organization that he began to think about his own potential biases. Justin's experience reflects predominant sociological theories, which posit that cross-racial contact is essential for changing racial attitudes (Pettigrew 1998). That is, although Justin may have had some exposure to information about race and racism through his college classes and his environment growing up, it was not until he formed cross-racial friendships that he was able to more fully understand and acknowledge that information, perhaps because this personal connection provided him with the motivation to do so (McClelland and Linnander 2006).

Whereas participants like Justin came to understand the nature of race and discrimination through questioning and deconstructing stereotypes and biases that they may hold, for others, the ability to view racial discrimination up close through the experiences of their Greek brothers and sisters was key in understanding the salience of race. Bradley, the white fraternity member, had one of these experiences, explaining:

> I think with the people that I've been able to connect with, them sharing their perspectives on something has totally, totally changed my view on how race is still a problem a lot of the times, or how races are treated differently.

Bradley's exposure to his fraternity brothers' very personal stories of how race had impacted their lives changed how he had originally conceived of discrimination. Again, close personal relationships across the color-line led to some white BGLO members' understanding of racial inequality.

These personal connections allowed white members a different way of understanding and interpreting racial issues, even if those issues were not necessarily happening to their brothers or sisters. For example, Emma, a 23-year-old white woman, explained that her sorority membership impacted how she understood race, saying that it "made [her] more aware of different racial issues that are going on." Emma's years in college, and her first years of membership in a BGLO, corresponded to a unique period when race-related instances dominated many news cycles and drew mainstream attention from the American public. She recounts: "Recently with all the tensions with Mike Brown and the Ferguson case, and all these other various things that are going on throughout the nation … That was something that I don't think I ever really paid attention to before."

In August 2014, Darren Wilson, a white police officer, in Ferguson, Missouri, shot Michael Brown, an unarmed Black teenager. Brown's death sparked weeks of protests in Ferguson. Despite the Missouri governor declaring a state of emergency and deploying the National Guard, protests continued. In November 2014, a grand jury decided against indicting Wilson, reigniting protests in Ferguson and across the U.S. The case also spurred a federal investigation by the Department of Justice. In the report, issued in March 2015, the Department of Justice called on Ferguson, Missouri to overhaul its criminal justice system, citing widespread racial bias throughout the police force and court system (for a detailed timeline of events, see Brown 2015).

Similarly, Chris, the white member, credits his BGLO membership with his ability to recognize the frequency of racial discrimination, drawing a comparison with other whites who have not joined Black organizations:

> I've noticed that there definitely is a lot of discrimination, and, I've noticed that even on our campus, a lot of the white people on our campus try to defend that there isn't discrimination. And I guess I might see it the way they do if I wasn't immersed in my community that I am in. Now, I see that there definitely is.

These responses from white BGLO members point to the lack of meaningful conversations about race and racism these individuals were exposed to before joining their respective organizations. Due to socialization as a white person into a society that downplays the widespread nature of racism, many white individuals arrive at college with an understanding that racism is no longer relevant, and that talking about race may be passé. Adam, the white fraternity member, explained that during his time in a BGLO:

> I think that was something that I learned is that you know when people say, "Oh, color doesn't matter" and you know, these things and it's you know nine times out of ten in my experience, anecdotally speaking it's some white person who's saying, "I don't care about color." And that's fine, you may not care about color but lots of people do and you have the luxury of not caring about your color. That's part of white privilege. We have the luxury of not caring about our color because it doesn't affect us.

Interestingly, these notions of colorblindness that Adam refers to actually drove many of our participants to join their BGLO, especially those who identified as white. However, we found that it was hard for non-Black members to maintain notions of colorblindness once fully immersed within a Black organization. Through the affective ties generated by their BGLO membership, these white BGLO members were able to broach topics of race and racism and reconsider long-held beliefs that they might have had before joining.

White BGLO members were not the only ones who had their under-standings of race and discrimination changed by the personal connection that they formed within their Black Greek organizations. Latino and Asian BGLO members also described these cross-racial friendships as eye-opening and infor-mative, even though many had joined their BGLO with an understanding of the importance of race and discrimination in society. Binh, the Vietnamese member, explained:

> I got to see first-hand [in my BGLO] the racism towards African American males … I'll walk with my fraternity brothers on our predominantly white campus. It's in a predominantly Black area, so we have police that drive around and stuff like that. So I'm walking with my fraternity brothers, and it's cold outside, you wear hoodies. And then they pull us over or they'll stop us while we're walking, [and ask] "Can we see IDs?" But I've done it tons of times and I've never gotten carded for my ID. But if I'm walking with my fraternity brother who happens to be Black who's wearing a hoodie, you know, they'll get stopped.

Even though Binh identifies as a person of color, his describes his experiences with police as very different from those of his Black brothers. These differences in police interactions across racial groups may make it more difficult for non-Blacks to empathize with Blacks as they call for overhauls to racialized policing practices. In fact, research finds that about 50 percent of whites but 84 percent of Blacks believe that Blacks in the U.S. are treated less fairly than whites in dealing with the police (Pew Research Center 2016). When asked the same question in regard to dealing with the police in their own communities, 34 percent of whites and 74 percent of Blacks stated that Blacks are treated less fairly than whites in their community (Pew Research Center 2016). Binh's excerpt underscores differential police interactions by race but also racialized policing practices. Because his campus is predominantly white but located in a predominantly Black area, the campus and police take extra precautions to protect its white students. In this excerpt, Binh and his fraternity brothers are racially profiled by police. They are assumed not to be college students but rather Black men against whom (white) college students must be protected. Binh's BGLO membership allowed him a personal connection that showcased the contours of difference in the types of racism between groups of color in the United States. Bailey, a 24-year-old sorority member of mixed Latina and white heritage, described how her BGLO mem-bership expanded her understandings of race and discrimination that might be specific to other cultures outside her own, explaining:

> It definitely made me a little more sensitive to the issues that other cultures face and it made me look more at what I'm saying and doing that could make somebody feel uncomfortable about that.

For the non-Black BGLO members we spoke with, their personal connections with their Black brothers and sisters changed the way that they understood how race and discrimination functioned in society. In particular, being with their Black friends as they recounted and experienced racism seemed to change how our respondents conceived of race in society. We found this was particularly true for white BGLO members who may have had limited exposure to cross-racial personal connections. Black friendships also enhanced the understanding of non-Black BGLO members of color of how racism, especially for Black individuals, works in the contemporary era. Our respondents' changing attitudes and deepened understanding of contemporary racism underscores an important element of cross-racial alliance. Without a belief in the persistence of racism or empathy with people of color, specifically Black Americans, then it is unlikely that whites and other non-Blacks would support efforts to dismantle discriminatory policies and practices.

Understanding Through Institutional Constraints

Although some participants utilized their cross-racial personal connections in order to shift their racial thinking, for other non-Black BGLO members, that shift came from experiences within the campus environment. For these members, it was not until they saw what they interpreted as discriminatory differences in treatment between their Black organizations and comparable white organizations on campus that they began to think about race and discrimination on a wider scale. Previous research has documented that institutions of higher education treat Black Greek organizations differently from their white counterparts. For example, Rashawn Ray and Jason Rosow (2012) highlighted how administrative forces hyper-focus on Black fraternities, cracking down on events, functions, and parties hosted by BGLOs, while there exists little accountability for white fraternities. Additionally, white fraternities are much more likely than Black fraternities to be institutionalized parts of student life – for example, having an on-campus fraternity house.

Amber, the white sorority member, recounted how noticing these institutional differences enhanced her understanding of race and discrimination overall:

> There was still so many racial barriers on campus that I think had I not been part of that [BGLO] I wouldn't have realized. I mean I have a lot of Black friends, and I've immersed myself in that culture, but I really didn't understand racism until I had to see it from that point of view and actually try to get things accomplished as a minority organization.

For Amber, even though she had "a lot of Black friends" and had been "immersed" in "that culture," it was not until she was facing institutional racial barriers that she was able to truly understand racism. Todd, the Mexican-Japanese fraternity member, recounted similar experiences at his private university, around how white and Black organizations were treated:

The white parties, the white people at our school, they all have their own lounges or houses, and they throw parties in their lounges and houses, and their lounges are on campus, but you'll never see a police officer at any of the white parties' lounges. The white people are allowed to do what they want, when they want. And it seems like they have no consequences. But at the Black parties, we have to have, we have to have them in one location. We have to have a certain capacity or number of people that is monitored. We have to have at least, I believe, it's now 15 police present at our parties in order for it to be run. And for any little thing, they'll shut down our party, and I just find that, so, it's so bizarre to actually think that only the Black students and Black parties have to have that and not the white students and white parties. That was a sign of racism that I've definitely seen.

Todd described an unequal system of institutional responses to Black organizations that impacted how he understood and interpreted his college campus. If one is specifically seeking out examples of unequal racial treatment in institutions of higher education, they are fairly easy to find given the recent high-profile conversations around racialized interactions with professors, protests about racial issues, and racist vandalism. However, for many non-Black BGLO members, it was not until they were part of a specific racialized organization on campus that they began to spot these instances of unequal treatment on campus.

Audra, a 21-year-old white sorority member, suggested that her BGLO membership provided her with the ability to recognize racial disparities within multiple contexts, such as on her private university campus. She says that her BGLO had "definitely given me some tools to really analyze what exactly is going on in the micro-culture of my university."

Through BGLO membership, non-Black BGLO members gained a more nuanced understanding of how race and discrimination functioned on their college campus. For these members, personal connections alone were not responsible for the shifts that they experienced in conceptualizing race and discrimination. Instead, a different understanding of racism was achieved when they understood how race functioned within an institutional context. This reflects a shift in our participants from conceptualizing racism as an interpersonal bias to thinking of racism as embedded in structures and institutions throughout society. By understanding themselves as part of an organization that was explicitly Black, our non-Black respondents realized the scope of institutional discrimination entrenched on their college campus.

Our respondents' understanding of institutionalized discrimination activated by their BGLO membership is an important outcome given that beliefs about racial equality differ widely by race. A national survey conducted by the Pew Research Center found that 88 percent of Black Americans, but only 53 percent of whites, believe that more needs to be done to ensure Blacks have equal rights (Pew Research Center 2016). Pew survey respondents were also split along racial lines on reasons for this inequality. Blacks were more likely than whites to cite discrimination (70 percent vs. 36 percent), poor-quality schools (75 percent vs. 53 percent), and lack of jobs (66 percent vs. 45 percent) (Pew Research Center 2016). We asked our respondents, "How much discrimination against Blacks do you feel there is in the United States today, limiting their chances to get ahead," among a series of other race-related questions (see Methodological Appendix). Response options were a lot, some, just a little, and none at all. Some 62 percent of our respondents overall and 69 percent of our white respondents answered "a lot," with several respondents going into detail about the importance of understanding racial discrimination and its far-reaching impacts.

These findings raise questions about how racial equality can be achieved when, in general, whites do not believe racial inequality exists. As the responses in this section demonstrate, through their BGLO membership, respondents gained both analytic tools and vocabulary to identify and understand racist incidents that occurred to their Black brothers and sisters, as well as to their fraternity or sorority. This was because their membership, through their personal connections that they developed and the new attention to institutional racism that it afforded, spurred a new level of introspection and reflexivity. As the next section shows, respondents also encountered experiences that shifted their understandings of their racial identities.

"I Didn't Just Stop at Learning African American History": Redefining Racial Identity

Along with providing non-Black BGLO members with the analytic tools to understand and identify race discrimination on their campus and in society, more broadly, BGLOs also led respondents to reform their interpretations of their own racial identities. This redefinition happened through their reflections and interactions regarding their experiences as non-Black people in a Black organization. For non-Black members of color, who often felt marginalized within their college environments because they did not identify as Black or white, their membership in a BGLO challenged them to understand and formulate their own racial identities. Some explained that their experiences within their Black Greek organizations caused them to feel tokenized, whereas others stated that it enhanced their own non-Black racial identity. Similarly, white individuals in BGLOs found that their association with Blackness via their membership caused them to reflect upon their racial identity, often for the first time in their lives.

Non-Black Tokens

One of the ways that non-Black members' racial identities were strengthened and redefined was through understanding of how their race related to their Greek organization. For some members, this was the first time that their racial identity stood in contrast to those with whom they surrounded themselves. Sometimes, being one of the only non-Black Greeks in their organization led to feeling tokenized. For example, Jasmine, a 32-year-old Puerto Rican and Korean sorority member, explained her sisters' responses when she performed in step routines with them, saying, "When I'm stepping, they'll be like, 'Oh you can step for an Asian.' And I'm like, 'How does an Asian step?'" Similarly, John, a 30-year-old Korean member of a fraternity explained:

> I think if anything people are, particularly because I was in a Black organization, a lot of the Black individuals felt that they had the ability to not be racist and they could say things such as calling me names of famous Asian people such as Jackie Chan or Yoko Ono and just thinking that was passable and appropriate behavior. I remember I had ordered just cheap delivery Chinese food and I was eating it in the living room of the [fraternity] room with chopsticks one evening and one of my prophytes walks in, who also lived in the house, and goes, "Yo, you look real Asian right now. I often forget that you are but right now, wow."

For some non-Black BGLO members, their experiences highlighted the racial differences between themselves and their brothers and sisters. Even though BGLOs are dedicated to issues of racial equality and had the impact of raising members' consciousness around racial discrimination, these members still experienced tokenizing language and experiences within their organization. However, some non-Black members interpreted this tokenizing aspect as a positive force that helped them to further solidify and understand their own racial identity. For example, Kelly, the white sorority member, discussed the attention she receives when she goes to national conferences or meetings as a white member of her historically Black sorority, saying, "Everyone wants a picture with the white [sorority member]." Kelly, however, sees this attention because she is a white member of a Black sorority as having a strengthening aspect on her own identity. She explained: "And it's like I'm ok with that because I understand. I get it. I know what I'm a member of."

Additionally, Thomas, a 26-year-old Filipino and Vietnamese fraternity member, explained that this tokenizing effect can actually have positive networking and relational impacts:

> It doesn't hurt to be like, you know, usually one of the only Asian American [members] in the room. It actually became pretty advantageous. People recognize me and remember me. They know that I'm interested in working in education, so they connect me with people that are educators. It became actually pretty easy to network and to navigate.

For these members, the tokenizing aspects of being one of the only non-Black people in the room helped them to experience their racial identity in new and different ways.

Racial Identity Spillover for People of Color

Even though BGLOs as organizations were created with the goal of providing a space to form and strengthen a positive Black identity, we find that they have a spillover effect in which other types of racial identities are reinterpreted, reformed, and strengthened. Through conversations with their cross-racial peers and programming that underscored the meaning of race in the United States, even non-Black BGLO members were forced to understand how they fit into the wider racial landscape. For many of the non-Black BGLO members of color that we talked to, this spillover effect was drawn from their personal connections between their BGLO brothers and sisters. Although feeling a bond with cross-racial friends and so much attention on the importance of Blackness and Black identities in society might be thought of as leading to a dismissal of other non-white, non-Black BGLO members, we found that many reported that their racial identity was strengthened through their Black organization. For example, Thomas explains:

> In terms of my racial identity, I actually became more racially aware of my own self and my own Asian American identity through [my fraternity]. I guess through understanding the perspectives of my Black fraternity brothers. To me it, I guess, it was equipping me with like the racial vernacular and the tools to understand what it means to be an Asian American in America.

Thomas credits his BGLO membership and the relationships with his fraternity brothers with an expanded awareness of his Asian American identity. Through his membership he gained analytic tools and language to critically investigate how Asian Americans are conceptualized within the United States.

Similarly, Todd, the Mexican-Japanese fraternity member, describes how BGLO membership changed how he identified: "Before, I would identify with more of my ethnicity being Mexican and Japanese, but now I just identify as a minority in whole, because I don't feel I'm any different than the Black students on campus or any other non-Caucasian student that I am faced with." For Todd, his BGLO membership allowed him to develop an idea of linked fate between himself and other individuals of color in society (Dawson 1995).

Beyond general awareness about their racial identity, the non-Black BGLO members that we talked to described how BGLO membership provided them with a method and motivation to explore their own ethnic heritage. Roano, the Puerto Rican fraternity member, stressed that his BGLO membership has been central to his development of his ethnic history:

> It's given me the opportunity to explore history, legacy from different perspectives. I didn't just stop at learning African American history. It ignited me to think about my legacy and history as Puerto Rican, my legacy and history as a member of the Latino community.

Likewise, Keilana, a 28-year-old Laotian sorority member said:

> Now more so than ever, I have a desire to learn about where my parents come from and as well as learning the language. I love the food but it's like, whenever I have kids I want to be able to teach them about the heritage and where we come from.

As Keilana's experience highlights, though BGLOs were initially created with the goal of providing a space that would enhance the development of a positive Black identity, the practices in place have a spillover effect in which she now has a stronger desire to explore her Laotian heritage.

Racial Identity Spillover: Becoming White

BGLOs also allowed white members to think about how their racial identity has impacted their experience. Bradley, the white fraternity member, linked his BGLO membership to transforming how he understood his own racial identity. He explained:

> I identify as white. I would say though that that means something very different than it did a year ago when I was starting my process. My whiteness is much more apparent to me and I'm much more aware of the implications that it has than before I started.

Whiteness is distinct from other races in its invisibility yet centrality throughout U.S. society. For example, George Lipsitz (1998:1) argued that despite the prevalence of whiteness in U.S. culture, it can be thought of as an invisible racial category, an "unmarked category against which difference is constructed." That is, as whiteness is normative in our society, it is often assumed. Race becomes a synonym for "non-white" and white people are seen as almost raceless or without a racial identity or ethnicity. Bradley's experience reflects this invisibility. Before joining his BGLO, Bradley did not consider his racial identity as white or the implications of being white when going about his life. Being white was not "apparent" to him. However, after becoming a member of a BGLO, Bradley's whiteness became much more central to how he understood himself.

Like Bradley, for many of the white respondents, joining and participating in a BGLO was really the first time that they remember their whiteness being perceived of as an important or meaningful identity marker. Audra, the white sorority member, described this phenomenon: "I think joining [my sorority] was a time that my white racial identity was very important. Other than that I think, I can't really say that it's been important because to be white in this country generally is to be what is accepted as the norm."

Samantha, a 22-year-old white sorority member, also experienced this shift from white racial identity being invisible and unacknowledged to being hyper-visible:

> [Joining my sorority] was the biggest like culture shock for me I guess you'd have to say 'cause I was submersed in it, like you know submersion. That makes you really question yourself ... I guess that's what made me most aware of like my identity with going through with [my sorority], because before this, I never had to question it. Being white, those are the only times I really thought about it. And I guess that's what helped me grow.

As these excerpts demonstrate, through their BGLO membership, non-Black respondents gained a more nuanced understanding of their own racial identity. In our racially segregated society, there is much controversy around organizations and groups that the public may interpret as promoting intra-racial divisions and associations, such as BGLOs. Often, the idea is that these organizations may cause further racial strain and may discount or erase the identities of non-Black interracial individuals who choose to participate within them. However, we found that the opposite seems to be true in BGLOs. BGLO membership caused non-Black members to confront their racial identity in new ways through interrogating their own assumptions about themselves and others, reflexivity about the effects of their words and actions, and exploration of their ethnic heritage.

"First, Be a Man": Affirming Gender Identity

Reconsidering and redefining how non-Black BGLO members considered their race was not the only impact on their identities that respondents reported. As BGLOs are both gender-specific and raced organizations, they provide members with understandings of how race and gender are connected and overlapping. Each organization aims to instill their members with their own particular conceptualization of what Black masculinity or femininity entails through standards, traditions, and community service projects. For example, Black sororities emerged as part of a movement to counter dominant notions of sexual and immoral Black femininity by showcasing respectable, educated, and community-minded black women. Membership in Alpha Kappa Alpha Sorority, Incorporated provided women with the know-how to fit into ideals of Black womanhood (Whaley 2010). Our participants also reported that pledging their organization helped them to affirm or reconsider their gender identities.

Some participants reported that the gendered aspect of the organization was especially important to them because they were non-Black members who did not initially understand or bond over issues of Black uplift. However, as men or women, they were able to transcend the color-line and participate in a fraternal organization that they felt enhanced their gender identity. For example, Emma, the white sorority member, explained that her perceptions of the gendered nature of the organization helped her to get over any barriers or misgivings she may have had about the racial differences between herself and her sisters, saying, "I saw the girls of [my sorority] and they were doing the community service aspect and they were very friendly, I really felt like they exhibited what I've been raised to believe a lady was." Through their dedication to community service and their pleasant nature, Emma felt that she was able to respect the women of her sorority and develop a strong bond with them.

However, it was not just that ideals of gender provided an initial bond or mutual respect for non-Black BGLO members. Through the activities provided by the organizations, our participants were able to refine their gender identity to more fully match with the ideas of organizational womanhood or manhood. In many BGLOs, ideas of masculinity and femininity are built into the mission statements of the organization, which were used to affirm and solidify respondents' gender identity and what actions they should partake in as a brother or sister of their organization. Antonio, a 24-year-old Mexican fraternity member, explains that his organization has a founding principle that emphasizes 'manhood.' He said, "It kind of like gave me like a guide to like actually make it through college like, you know, first, be a man. I feel like it's kind of given me those guides and those rules to actually live by."

Other participants talked about how formative their BGLO was to forming their gender identity. Roano, the Puerto Rican fraternity member, discussed how being in a BGLO allowed him to explore the meaning and possibilities for masculinity:

> So my second year of college, my father decided to leave our family. He divorced my mom. And I think I went through some, some crisis of masculinity, crisis of identity. When I made the decision to join the fraternity, I think a part of it was also me trying to connect to male figures, not necessarily to replace my father, but to reinforce and help me make sense of what it means to be a man of your word, what it means to be an honorable individual, how do you develop that identity in the community. Because of, you know, the way that NPHC works, we are very connected to our alumni chapters, I had great role models that were husbands and fathers, professional men that were able to help me manage that very traumatic experience in my life.

Roano was able to use the connections he built through his BGLO to help him think through and define how to be a man in society, and find refuge in a confusing time that challenged his gender identity. For many respondents, they counted their brothers and sisters as role models for how to perform a positive masculinity or femininity, especially for members of color.

Other respondents recalled how their BGLO membership allowed them to develop relationships with their brothers and sisters that were different from the other types of friendships that they had established in their lives. Keilana, the

Laotian sorority member, described, "I grew up with a lot of guys. I have two brothers. I'm the only girl. In an Asian household, it's pretty strict. I don't talk about relationships or anything with my parents. So it was an outlet. It was a group of women I can speak to and call my sisters." For Keilana, her relationships with her sisters were unique amongst the other relationships in her life and provided an outlet to align herself with women.

Similarly, John, the Korean BGLO fraternity member, explained that their experience in their fraternity allowed them to explore their identity as gender non-conforming, and to explore and establish friendships with men:

> I felt that Greek life was an opportunity to kind of almost have a structured interface with other individuals, particularly individuals who identified as men. In my life, I had many working, functional, and long-lasting relationships with women. That's who I kind of grew up with as friends. That's who I associated with easily in high school and in my initial days at [my university]. It was more so challenging to create and cultivate those long-lasting relationships with men.

Although John was able to create friendships with "individuals who identified as men," thereby allowing John to expand his own conceptions of masculinity, John's fraternity did not allow for a reformation of their personal gender identity.

> But I feel like, even the set-up of fraternities and sororities based on a dichotomous view of gender which is often conflated with sex is something that is not something that I stand for nor representative of me and my identity. It's challenging to say I am a [fraternity] man when I may not even want to associate with the label of man.

While fraternity membership initially served as an important space for John to understand gendered identities, there were firm limits to what role the fraternity as a traditional, gender-conforming environment could play in John's own continued gendered expression.

For non-Black members of BGLOs, the centrality of gender in their organization was something that was used to bridge the racial divide that they were crossing. They used commonalities that they found with their Black brothers and sisters to downplay any racial differences that may exist between them. Additionally, the gendered nature of the organization provided participants with new ways of thinking and refining their gender identities and developing important gendered relationships in their lives that they felt were lacking. The gendered nature of their participation, however, was contained within a specific type of gendered expression, namely "proper" womanhood and manhood. In short, this gendered nature that respondents felt drawn to and were expected to portray reflect the politics of respectability, the strategies and values created in the early nineteenth century and enacted to combat dominant narratives about the immorality of Black people (Higginbotham 1994). Within their founding and early decades, BGLOs drew upon respectability politics to advance the Black community, and this ideology continues to persist in BGLOs today (for an analysis of respectability politics in Alpha Kappa Alpha, see Whaley 2010). In particular, respectability is evidenced through the affirmation of hegemonic masculinity within Black Greek-letter fraternities, as our male respondents underscore.

Conclusion

Crossing the color-line into Black Greek organizations has the potential to challenge notions about race and association. In BGLOs, symbolic racial boundaries function within the ways that non-Black members conceptualize their entrance into these socially and culturally rich spaces steeped in Black history. Interestingly, non-Black members did not always frame themselves as traversing an important or meaningful boundary in society. In a society where people are increasingly told that race is no longer a meaningful barrier to equal life outcomes, many individuals are able to avoid or ignore the implications of the color-line.

By purposefully joining an organization that resides across racial boundaries, non-Black members must make sense of how to understand their racial organization within a supposedly "post-racial" world. As we uncovered, some of these members did so by using their membership to bolster claims of colorblindness. For others, the boundary into BGLOs was stark and salient, and they approached crossing it with a variety of strategies that emphasized previous boundary transgressors and role models, the importance of desegregation, and emphasizing a linked fate between their racial identities and Blackness.

Entering the symbolic boundaries of BGLOs impacted how non-Black members came to understand and conceptualize racial issues and racism in the United States. For non-Black members, the personal connections that they developed across the racial line and the experience of being a member of a racialized institution allowed them to acknowledge the reality of race in ways that they had not previously been able to do. This was particularly pronounced for white BGLO members, who reported that they had not considered the contours of race in the United States until their experience in their Black Greek organization aided them in doing so.

However, acknowledgment and understanding of how race functioned in society was not the only way that crossing the symbolic boundary of racial associations impacted the members that we talked to. We found that their roles as non-Black members of Black organizations worked to refine and retool their identities. In particular, their association with Blackness, which was often used to differentiate and distinguish their own racial identities and experiences, impacted the racial identities of non-Black members. Sometimes experiencing a tokenizing effect within their Black Greek organizations highlighted these differences. For white BGLO members, this meant acknowledging and conceptualizing themselves as white, even when they had not previously thought about their place in the racial landscape. For members of color, the community developed around strengthening Black identities had a spillover effect which also strengthened their own racial identities. Of course, Black Greek organizations are also gendered organizations, and many of the members we talked to described how their membership also worked to strengthen their gender identities and gendered relationships.

Our conversations with non-Black members demonstrate the boundary and identity work that takes place when individuals cross the color-line. Given the race-based social setting of BGLOs, it is not surprising that we find that much of the boundary and identity work that these non-Black members report is spurred by relational influences. Indeed, racial identities and boundaries are often formulated in relations and comparison to other individuals. In the next chapter, we explore how non-Black BGLO members conceptualized their membership as part of a larger campus environment and racial landscape. In doing so, we examine how racial boundaries are created, enforced, and transformed.

References

Bonilla-Silva, Eduardo. 2010. *Racism Without Racists: Color-Blind Racism & Racial Inequality in Contemporary America*, 3rd Ed. Lanham, MD: Rowman & Littlefield.

Brown, Emily. 2015. "Timeline: Michael Brown shooting in Ferguson, Mo." *USA Today*, August 10. Retrieved from www.usatoday.com/story/news/nation/2014/08/14/michael-brown-ferguson-missouri-timeline/14051827/.

Dawson, Michael C. 1995. *Behind the Mule: Race and Class in African-American Politics*. Princeton, NJ: Princeton University Press.

Gallagher, Charles A. 2003. "Color-Blind Privilege: The Social and Political Functions of Erasing the Color Line in Post Race America." *Race, Gender, & Class* 10(4):22–37.

Higginbotham, Evelyn Brooks. 1994. *Righteous Discontent: The Women's Movement in the Black Baptist Church, 1880–1920*. Cambridge, MA: Harvard University Press.

Hughey, Matthew W. 2008. "'I Did it for the Brotherhood': Nonblack Members in Black Greek-Letter Organizations." Pp. 313–343 in *Black Greek-Letter Organizations in the 21st Century*, edited by G.S. Parks. Lexington, KY: University Press of Kentucky.

Lamont, Michele, and Marcel Fournier. 1992. "Introduction." Pp. 1–16 in *Cultivating Differences: Symbolic Boundaries and the Making of Inequality*, edited by M. Lamont and M. Fournier. Chicago: University of Chicago Press.

Lipsitz, George. 1998. *The Possessive Investment In Whiteness: How White People Profit From Identity Politics*. Philadelphia: Temple University Press.

McClelland, Katherine, and Erika Linnander. 2006. "The Role of Contact and Information in Racial Attitude Change among White College Students." *Sociological Inquiry* 76(1):81–115.

Pettigrew, Thomas F. 1998. "Intergroup Contact Theory." *Annu Rev Psychol* 49:65–85.

Pew Research Center. 2016. "On Views of Race and Inequality, Blacks and Whites Are Worlds Apart." Pew Research Center, June 27. Retrieved from www.pewsocialtrends.org/2016/06/27/3-discrimination-and-racial-inequality/.

Ray, Rashawn and Jason Rosow. 2012. "The Two Different Worlds of Black and White Fraternity Men: Visibility and Accountability as Mechanisms of Privilege." *Journal of Contemporary Ethnography* 41(1):66–94.

Small, Mario Luis, David J. Harding, and Michele Lamont. 2010. "Reconsidering Culture and Poverty." *The ANNALS of American Academy of Political and Social Science* 629(1):6–27.

Warikoo, Natasha K. 2010. "Symbolic Boundaries and School Structure in New York and London Schools." *American Journal of Education* 116(3):423–451.

Whaley, Deborah Elizabeth. 2010. *Disciplining Women: Alpha Kappa Alpha, Black Counterpublics, and the Cultural Politics of Black Sororities.* Albany, NY: State University of New York Press.

3

ON THE YARD

Race on the College Campus

> When I went to college, I felt more of a Black/white. You either hang out with the white kids or you're hanging out with the Black kids, one or the other because there's not a whole lot in between. So I did feel myself being more engaged with students that identified as Black and being more involved in activities that centered around that, although I was still very much, I think, I was very much aware of my Latino identity.
>
> *Osita, 33-year-old Puerto Rican sorority member*

Despite the integration of educational institutions and universities' commitments to campus diversity, students continue to feel a palpable Black–white racial divide on their college campuses. This divide leaves many students, like Osita, caught between the dichotomy of the color-line. How non-Black students and some white students navigate this racial divide and the role that Black Greek-letter organization (BGLO) membership plays is the focus of this chapter. In particular, we illuminate the relationship between context and group membership by showing how campus racial climate acts as a catalyst for membership in race-based organizations, like Black fraternities and sororities. We find that these organizations provide an important counter-space for our respondents, regardless of their racial identities. We also highlight non-Black BGLO membership as a particular case of a larger shift in racial understandings away from a Black–white racial binary to one dichotomizing whiteness as compared to non-whiteness. Therefore, we argue, BGLOs are able to facilitate members' understanding of their place within this shifting racial hierarchy.

Campus Racial Climate

The U.S. Department of Education reports the rates of racial harassment on college campuses has been steady over the past 25 years, with 146 incidents reported in 2015 (Griggs 2015). However, research suggests that only 13 percent of racial incidents are reported to campus authorities, suggesting that the problem may be more widespread than even acknowledged by campus authorities or reported in the media (Hurtado and Ruiz 2012). Recently, the U.S. witnessed a culmination of highly publicized racialized events and protests resulting in the University of Missouri's system president and the flagship campus chancellor stepping down amid criticism by students of gross inattention to racism. These ongoing racialized and racist incidents characterize and influence the campus racial climate that students experience. While students of various racial and ethnic groups experience the campus racial climate differently, research shows that all students, including whites, are affected by the campus racial climate (Gurin et al. 2002).

Campus racial climate comprises the norms, values, and routines of an institution's environment in regards to race (Chavous 2005). It is one component of the diversity of college campuses. Other elements include structural (such as campus composition), interactional (or opportunities to interact across race inside and outside the classroom), and curricular (including racial diversity within the curriculum) (Hall et al. 2011; Hurtado et al. 1998). Although each of these components is distinct, they are mutually reinforcing. Studies find wide-ranging benefits of campus diversity, whether social, academic, or co-curricular. In particular, studies find campus diversity linked to increased civic engagement and cultural awareness, and cultivating feelings of "authentic" belonging within the university (Bowman 2010, 2011; Hurtado 2005; Milem and Hakuta 2000; Milem et al. 2005).

However, these benefits only happen if universities are intentional about providing opportunities and spaces for meaningful cross-racial interaction starting when students first enter college (Antonio 2004; Ward and Zarate 2015; Warikoo and Deckman 2014). As such, numerical diversity is a necessary, but not sufficient, precondition for meaningful cross-racial interaction (Chang et al. 2004). In fact, universities with higher levels of racial diversity also often have campus conditions that reduce cross-racial interaction (Chang et al. 2004). As we discussed previously (see Introduction), instead of meaningful engagement with difference, universities often employ 'weak' diversity. This celebration of difference is often not met with structural, interactional, or curricular supports.

Perhaps because of the exposure to racial diversity in college, coupled with a campus racial climate that exalts "diversity" and "inclusion" even as campuses remain segregated, unequal, and havens for microaggressions, research finds racial identity a most salient outcome of campus contextual factors (Grasmuck and Kim 2010; Hurtado et al. 2015; Shiao and Tuan 2008). Given the focus on diversity initiatives, debates over college admissions and affirmative action, and race-related activism on college campuses, white students are also likely exposed to some level of discussion about race and their college life.

Shifting Racial Landscape on Campus

Traditionally, the Black–white experience marks the racial landscape. For instance, Charles Gallagher (1995), by engaging Peggy McIntosh's notion of white privilege, argues that collegiate whites are regularly invited to understand "race" through the lens of white/non-white competition for campus resources, such as scholarships, admission, campus spaces, and mentoring programs. In step with predominantly white institutions, majority white campus clubs and organizations, such as Greek-letter organizations, may facilitate these racial worldviews (Hughey 2010).

Recently, sociological research has called for attention to those who might fall in between or outside the Black–white racial binary. How scholars have conceptualized the position of other racial groups in the United States has varied. Some scholars conceptualize the racial landscape as a multi-layered racial hierarchy or racial continuum wherein other racial groups may act as honorary whites, such as being seen as a model minority (Bonilla-Silva 2004) or be triangulated as a racial group that falls somewhere between the dominance of whiteness and the subordination of Blackness (Kim 1999). Other scholars point out that Asians and Latinos often engage in and hold negative stereotypical views of Blacks and instead emphasize their commonality with whites (Lee and Bean 2004; McClain et al. 2006), and whites often view Asians and Latinos as more similar to them than Blacks (Gallagher 2004). This social distancing creates what can be thought of as a Black/non-Black racial divide in the United States (Warren and Twine 1997; Yancey 2003). Finally, other scholars postulate that it appears that there are certain conditions wherein people of color instead emphasize connectedness among non-whites, particularly when faced with similar types of discrimination or social isolation (Chutuape 2016; Kaufmann 2003). This kind of connectivity among people of color suggests a white/non-white racial binary may be another way to understand the racial landscape of the United States.

The larger debates in the sociological literature around which model of racial hierarchy fits the contemporary racial landscape the best raises questions about how racial stratification manifests on the contemporary college campus. Despite university claims of the importance of diversity, students find those claims do not often materialize (Harper and Hurtado 2007). In response to unwelcoming and alienating campus climates, as well as discriminatory and racist experiences, students of color often create their own counter-spaces (Solorzano et al. 2000). Racial and ethnic-specific organizations have been shown to provide students of color the opportunity to express and develop their racial identities, provide opportunities to engage in community service activities, advocate for their ethnic communities via institutional change, and connect with other students of their racial group (Harper and Quaye 2007; Inkelas 2004; Museus 2008). Pan-ethnic, multiracial, and multicultural organizations also provide students from multiple racial backgrounds the chance to come together to develop opportunities to engage in cross-racial discussions, participate in multicultural community service activities, and lessen racial divisions on campus (McCabe 2011). These student organizations also indicate how the racial hierarchy functions on college campuses, wherein students from various racial backgrounds, despite assumptions that different racial groups may have unique or separate interests on campus, feel a sense of linked fate that draws them together (Dawson 1994). One such student organization that cultivates a sense of linked fate is BGLOs.

Going Greek: Response to a White/Non-White Divide

Given the overt racialization of BGLOs, how our non-Black participants came to identify and join these organizations provides insight into the larger campus racial culture. From our members' responses we find multiple iterations of racial divides depending on the context. Whether they attended small liberal arts schools with few non-white students or large public institutions with larger numbers of students from multiple non-white racial and ethnic groups, respondents encountered racially-based campus divides. About half of the respondents commented that they felt fellow students and faculty made no distinctions between the various students of color. Respondents drew comparisons to the diversity they experienced prior to college and the lack of diversity or, as Adam, a 39-year-old white fraternity member who joined a graduate chapter, described, the "severe divide" they were faced with in college, describing their initial reactions as "culture shock." Khashifa, a 35-year-old Pakistani sorority member at a large private university, stated: "The campus at that time, was very divided ... The environment was very divided. It was, you were either white or you were Black. You were not anything in between."

The sentiment of experiencing a Black–white divide was echoed across respondents regardless of when they attended college. This racially divided environment led to respondents' understanding of a distinct racial hierarchy. In many cases, respondents reported a rethinking of their own racial identity and where they fit in on their college campus. John, a 30-year-old Korean fraternity member, who identified as gender non-conforming and attended a large private university, explained how the campus racial climate affected the decision to join a National Pan-Hellenic Council (NPHC) organization and John's own understanding of their racial identity:

> There was either join white or join Black and while I didn't identify as Black, I felt far more comfortable in Black social environments and around a lot of my Black friends. So, that's kind of like what pushed me into that. Knowing that I identified at least as a person of color, I felt like my experience could be more, I guess, even affirmed through the joining of an NPHC organization than any others.

For respondents like John, who were neither white nor Black, they had to find connections with other racial group members in order to find a sense of belonging on campus. Their own racial group membership or experiences were not integrated into their college campus. The feeling of being either/or left our Asian and Latino respondents in a precarious position. Echoing John's statement was Todd, a 20-year-old Mexican-Japanese fraternity member enrolled at a small private university, who stated:

> So me just being a minority in itself, I knew I would be better off joining a minority Greek-letter organization. And, at our school we don't have any other minority Greek organizations. You're either in a Black fraternity or in a white fraternity as we would say.

Both John and Todd underscore the persistent racial boundaries in collegiate fraternal organizations, and the conundrum for students who fall outside the Black–white divide. Facing an alienating campus racial climate and the flattening of identities of students of color, John and Todd identified BGLOs as a safe racial space, although the space might not be originally designed to represent them. While these responses indicate the unspoken racial rules for membership, particularly in white fraternal organizations, Sri, a 37-year-old Bangladeshi fraternity member at a large public university, expanded on this idea, explaining how he believed he would have been received in a white organization: "Here's the thing, I felt like I would've been a token [if I had joined a historically white fraternity] … You didn't have just a lot of diversity in the white organizations. It didn't happen."

Interestingly, while being a racial token in a white fraternity was enough of a concern for Sri to avoid pledging one, he did not have the same concerns about joining a BGLO as the only Bangladeshi fraternity member. Later in the interview, he stated that although there were no other non-Black members in BGLOs on his campus at the time he joined, he still felt that he was included as a full member. In other words, he was neither alienated nor exoticized because of his racial differences within BGLOs, although he suspected he would have been in a white fraternity. Research provides evidence of Sri's suspicions. In a study of non-white members of traditionally white fraternities and sororities, Hughey (2010) finds that in order to be accepted as full members, non-white members are often expected to fulfill stereotypical roles. These roles include expectations about their background and family structure, interests, and serving as the diversity position in their organization. Though, as we discuss in Chapter 2, similar tokenizing dynamics can also exist for non-Black members in BGLOs.

Like Sri, many of our respondents identified BGLOs as providing a space to develop a sense of inclusion and feeling that one was an integral part of a community. For example, Bailey, a 24-year-old white-Hispanic sorority member at a large public university explains:

But what I really did like about my campus, the minority community is very close knit because it's so small. Everybody knows everybody. You don't walk by somebody without saying hello. And that's another part of what really drew me to being a part of that community.

Another member characterized the campus as "an HBCU within a PWI." The idea of the minority student population as a historically black college or university (HBCU) within a predominantly white institution (PWI), clearly illustrates the complexity of the success of integration within higher education. Non-white students feel alienated and unseen within the larger campus.

For some of our white respondents, the white/non-white divide was also apparent. Whereas a few explicitly identified the racially divided nature of their campus, others spoke in more coded language about how they were unsettled by the "mainstream culture" of their university. One of the most specific accounts of the divide by a white respondent was by Chris, a 22-year-old white fraternity member at a large public university, who described an event characterizing the campus climate stating "We've had recent things like [a white fraternity], they had a [racial stereotype-themed] party recently, and a lot of people are saying, 'Oh that's not racist.'" White fraternities hosting parties where attendees are encouraged to wear attire mocking ethnic cultures or racial groups are, unfortunately, more commonplace than one might expect. Such parties are part of a long history of both racially discriminatory policies and practices within white fraternities and sororities as well as blackface minstrelsy itself (Patton 2008; Ross 2016). Although white fraternity chapters across the U.S. continue to be suspended, expelled, or otherwise sanctioned for their racist behavior, as the fraternity in Chris's excerpt was, for many students these events are seen as "not racist."

These responses show two important elements of contemporary college campuses. First, despite calls for inclusion and increased diversity, racial divides on college campuses persist. Weak diversity, though making the campus appear racially integrated, does not, in fact, lead to welcoming and affirming campus cultures for all students. Although our respondents referred to this divide along a white–Black line, analyzing their comments more in depth reveals this division more accurately can be thought of as separating white students from non-whites. This racial division emphasized a shared marginalization as students of color. Even students who identified as white noticed this divide, and those who were uncomfortable with it sought out ways to challenge it, such as joining BGLOs. Second, racial- and ethnic-based organizations continue to provide a counter-space to unwelcoming campus racial climates. Only 20 percent of our respondents reported any awareness of BGLOs prior to entering college, and only two of those respondents expressed that they had some interest in joining a BGLO prior to college. For the vast majority of our respondents, the shock of the divisive campus racial culture and the more welcoming and inclusive nature of BGLOs served as an impetus for membership.

Campus Racial Climate: Effects on BGLO Chapters

While the overall college campus climate was a primary reason why respondents found refuge in BGLOs, individual BGLO chapters facilitated their eventual membership. Some 56 percent of our respondents joined chapters that previously had non-Black members at some point in their chapter's history. Two respondents chartered the chapters at their schools. Among respondents who, to their knowledge, were the first non-Black member in their chapter's history, four respondents had other non-Black members join after them.

In the previous chapter, we detailed the type of color-line crossing respondents engaged in. However, it is important to note how the chapters themselves were also affected by the college racial composition and the inclusion of non-Black members. As John, the Korean fraternity member, explained, "the small population of Black individuals, particularly Black males at [the private university] … really just allowed or facilitated the inclusion of individuals of other races more easily than I think you may witness at other institutions." Khashifa, the Pakistani sorority member, also emphasized the small non-white population of students and correspondingly the limited number of organizations committed to social change:

> [O]n campus there was only a few organizations that were doing things in the benefit of minority community and that was either the Black Student Alliance or it was the Black Greeks on campus. And if you wanted to be a part of anything, you were going to join one of those organizations to try to influence change on campus. And so that's what started the decision to join a Greek organization.

As John and Khashifa highlight, the small number of non-white students led to the campus being organized around a white/non-white divide. In order to find a sense of belonging within this racial configuration, students of color identified with one another. Due to the small number of non-white students, their concerns were largely ignored within the broader campus culture. As a result, students of color participated in or created their own interest groups to address their needs. As Khashifa's excerpt indicates, these groups and BGLOs in particular were often the primary source of social justice programming for college campuses (for examples of historic and contemporary racial justice programming within BGLOs, see Chapter 1).

Even though the racially divided college campus acted as a push factor for our respondents to join BGLOs, they were not necessarily welcomed with open arms. In the next sections we discuss the types of boundary enforcement respondents experienced as a result of their color-line crossing. Here we highlight one example of two nearby chapters' approaches to non-Black interest in their BGLO. Hao, a 35-year-old Vietnamese fraternity member at a large public research university, shared his experience with pledging his fraternity:

[T]here was hesitation. You know, this chapter had never had anybody that was not Black that didn't look Black. So they've had like Puerto Ricans and [other] members but they tend to kinda look Black or can easily blend in, whereas I'm Asian American. I tend to stand out automatically the moment I even step foot into any setting. And so the conversations were very difficult, and they were like, "We have to make sure that we are investing in you as a fraternity member and that we can hold you down wherever we go." And so, they were very honest in saying that everybody in our fraternity may not look at this in a positive light. And so balancing those thoughts and, you know, my ambition to join something of this level and of this stature, that push or that desire outweighed the negative. So, I won't lie, it was a tough decision, once they actually decided that, ok, they're going to take a risk on me, you know, it then became incumbent upon me to really make sure that I had come in with the right attitude, the right information, and making sure that I could hold steadfast to what I believed in. So, it was tough.

Although Hao's chapter had previous non-Black members, as he explains, "they had never had anybody that was not Black that didn't look Black." Hao's membership would visibly disrupt the racial homogeneity of the chapter, a disruption the chapter was not prepared to address. In fact, Hao was initially rejected from joining. He explained this:

I actually decided, tried to join the fold my junior year and was not accepted the first time around, but then tried again my senior year, my first semester senior year actually was taken, and so I guess the rest is history after that point.

It is unclear from Hao's version of the events what changes may have happened among the chapter members that led to their decision to accept Hao as a member. However, transformations among the chapter members' attitudes are evident as they not only admitted Hao but also another visibly non-Black member, who was Latino. What is clear, though, is that even though there was a precedent, to some degree, for non-Black membership the inclusion of phenotypically non-Black members, especially an Asian American, was not a decision taken lightly. After all, even though the chapter eventually accepted him, Hao's chapter members were forthright in telling him that fraternity members at large "may not look at this in a positive light." The reaction of Hao's chapter members demonstrates the role of phenotype within the contours of racial group membership. Previous Latino members were racialized as Black, easily blending in with their fellow Black BGLO members. Hao's physical features visibly marked him as an outsider.

While Hao was the first non-Black member in his chapter's recent history and was greeted with hesitancy, a nearby college was more open to non-Black membership. Hao recalled a phone call he had from a fraternity brother, who was a member of the graduate chapter responsible for the nearby college's undergraduate chapter.

> I remember getting a phone call from one of the chapter brothers in the graduate chapter, and it was like, "Hey, hey we got a couple brothers here at [nearby college] that are looking to join the fraternity." And I was like, "Ok." "I want you to talk to them." I was like, "Oh ok. You know, no problem. Whatever." They're like, "But here's the kicker – they're Asian." I'm like, "Oh, that's cool." I was able to have conversations with some young men that were Asians and [who had] some hesitancies to join the fold of this fraternity. I was able to have conversations with those folks, and kinda give them my experiences and let them know that they'd always have a support system at least from me and some of my chapter brothers and brothers in this area. And so, I'm happy to say that now [that college] has had three Asian guys cross within their chapter within the past seven years. So, that's a lot. I mean, I'm the only one in my chapter but at [that college] you would have more of those non-Blacks, and so it's been pretty incredible to see that.

Where Hao's college was a large public research university, the nearby college was a small private liberal arts college. The smaller student population may have helped facilitate non-Black membership to some degree. Binh, a 29-year-old Vietnamese fraternity member at a small private liberal arts college describes the reception he received as the first non-Black member of his chapter.

> I think there was a little bit of friction … as an Asian American joining. At least I think that naturally people are a little bit more suspicious of why, which is kind of absurd … if you're for the larger the purpose, I think that should matter more. But once I was in, there's still a high level of scrutiny but the friction, the friction, at least in our chapter, of having people that come from different ethnic backgrounds or cultural backgrounds, was gone … there was one older fraternity member that was like not for it, not for it [allowing non-Black members] at all. And I think it took a while for that kind of credibility to build and so I think that's the kind of, at least at the chapter level, something that I brought … showing that people can be committed to an organization regardless of race was huge.

Binh points out the "friction" he received for joining and the intense level of scrutiny he received based on his race. His chapter members were suspicious as to why an Asian American would want to join a historically Black organization, especially one that continues to fight for racial uplift for the Black community. Though the friction and scrutiny were likely not only questions about his reason for joining, but also internal questions about if non-Black members should be allowed to join at all, Binh emphasizes that regardless of race, members should be scrutinized for their reason for seeking membership. Here he challenges the assumption of a lack of commitment to BGLOs and their mission of racial uplift based on race. In the end, Binh was pledged and believes that his membership was instrumental in demonstrating that "people can be committed to an organization regardless of race." Whether it was a result of his commitment, the support of other chapters' members, or other influences, his chapter continued to pledge non-Black members.

Thomas, a 26-year-old Vietnamese-Filipino fraternity member, who joined the chapter after Binh, explained:

> The racial and physical, like phenotypic makeup was of the chapter at the time, was still predominantly Black. I mean, Binh was the only non-Black member at the time. But, you know, the brothers, they didn't seem to make that a big deal.

For Thomas, he did not perceive his racial identity as a hindrance to his membership. In fact, he explained that he "always felt empowered to inform brothers when I feel that they're being offensive," though those moments "[don't] happen often if at all." As evidence of his full inclusion, Thomas was elected president of his chapter. Michael, a 22-year-old white fraternity member, who joined the chapter long after Binh graduated, described the more current state of the chapter:

> Each organization is pretty small. So, we have 13 members now on the yard ... There's actually at least one non-Black member represented through each [BGLO chapter at the college]. But I think we're the most diverse. We have – I'm white. We have one Latino American. We have an Asian American and two half-white members as well.

Binh's, Thomas's, and Michael's excerpts highlight how campus size, racial composition, and campus racial climate together affect individual BGLO chapters' membership. Through tracing the non-Black membership of this one chapter, we see the trajectory of non-Black membership. Binh became the first non-Black member in his chapter, but that chapter now is the most diverse BGLO chapter on campus, according to current member Michael. Moreover, each BGLO on campus has at least one non-Black member. This is likely facilitated by the campus size and campus climate at this small private school. Although each chapter may have non-Black members, it does not mean those members do not experience pushback, to which Hao's and Binh's excerpts allude.

Through the attempted crossing of the color-line, racial boundaries were contested and, to some degree, redrawn. Although we were not privy to the debates among the Black BGLO members in regard to Hao's or Binh's potential membership, their respective chapters' hesitation demonstrates the difficulty in crossing established racial lines. There is a suspicion rooted in historic race relations and perpetuated through contemporary racial discourse that positions marginalized racial groups against one another. Though these interested members were involved in other minority-interest organizations, Black-centered groups, and social justice work, joining a BGLO was perceived by some as a step too far. In the following sections, we delve deeper into the types of boundary enforcement respondents experienced and what it tells us about racial hierarchies.

Racial Boundary Enforcement: Revealing a More Complicated Racial Landscape

Although the white/non-white campus racial divide served as an impetus for coming to identify with and join a BGLO, the consequences of the color-line for our participants did not dissolve upon joining. Once members, they experienced both external and internal responses to their BGLO membership that aimed at condemning them for crossing racial boundaries. Both BGLO outsiders and insiders had responses to non-Black members, which provided respondents with the analytic tools to navigate the larger racial landscape and their place within it. These experiences as non-Black BGLO members led respondents to reform their interpretations of their racial identity. This external and internal racial boundary enforcement revealed a more complicated racial hierarchy than the white/non-white racial campus divide that participants originally experienced. For some participants, reactions from others, especially outsiders, highlighted a larger and more stratified racial landscape. Alternatively, for the white participants, the reactions to their membership provided further evidence for a white/non-white racial binary. Conversely, other participants found that others, especially their BGLO sisters and brothers, viewed their membership within a Black/non-Black racial hierarchy. We discuss these differences below.

Racial Boundary Enforcement: Racial Hierarchies

Despite the association of students of color that led to respondents characterizing their campuses as divided along a white/non-white line, once respondents were BGLO members, they became hyper-visible both because of their BGLO membership and their racial difference from most other BGLO members. Experiences of boundary enforcement, especially from white students, drew attention to a racial hierarchy, highlighting that respondents were behaving outside the expected norms for their racial group. In these instances, respondents shared how their decision to join a BGLO was deemed a racial transgression. For example, Bailey, the white-Hispanic sorority member, stated:

> And I just remember being there [at a campus fundraising event for all student organizations] and it was one of the first things that we did after we had

joined and we're wearing our letters and hanging out with our little groups and it's a room full of people and I just remember feeling like everybody that was white was staring at me and just looking at me crazy. And as I came to be involved in more things with the organization, I really came to feel like that more often because people would look at me like, "But what's she doing there with them. She doesn't fit in."... I know a lot of people questioned it [her BGLO membership] because I'm Caucasian and Hispanic. So a lot of people were like, "Why wouldn't you join one of the Hispanic organizations?"

The stares and critiques of white students exposed her racial transgressions, emphasizing that her BGLO membership was outside what was deemed appropriate behavior for her presumed race. The questioning of outsiders reveals both a form of the one-drop rule, where Bailey was racialized as Hispanic because of her white-Hispanic mixed-race heritage, as well as a distinct racial order, where some Latinos are privileged over Blacks.

Thomas, the Vietnamese-Filipino fraternity member, shared a similar experience: "If anything I received the most friction from white people who don't understand my decision, who you know said things like, 'Why are you trying to be Black?' or 'Why did you join a Black fraternity? Why couldn't you join another fraternity?'" In the contemporary racial landscape wherein Blackness is often delineated at the bottom of the racial hierarchy, whites viewed BGLO membership for non-Blacks as the last resort or a puzzling choice. The comment of "[w]hy couldn't you join another fraternity?" highlights the assumption that Asian Americans are, or should be, aligned with whites, or at the very least should not be aligned with Blacks. Thomas's BGLO membership is an affront to Asian American 'honorary whiteness,' whereby Asian Americans are idealized as 'white' because of their socioeconomic success, educational attainment, and cultural values vis-à-vis other racialized minority groups.

Other responses were subtler, yet still communicated that the respondent's BGLO membership was inappropriate for their ethnic background and revealed a more complicated racial hierarchy. Hao, the Vietnamese fraternity member, shared how administrators reacted to his membership:

Well I know administrators looked at me very differently because a lot [of] them didn't know that my interest lied in a fraternity because I had held so many leadership positions on campus. Our admin. team in student activities and the dean of students' office were very surprised when I decided to join the fold, and they were like, "I would've never guessed." And so, I was like, "Why?" You know, they're like, "You're just so mild mannered. And you're just kind of quiet." ... I guess they viewed fraternity life, and NPHC men to be very, to fit a certain mold, and evidently I didn't fit that mold.

These administrators' responses conveyed that not only was Hao acting outside what was appropriate for his ethnic group but also that there was an expected behavior for the typical (Black) NPHC man. Given that research finds BGLO fraternity and sorority members to be involved in multiple student organizations, often holding leadership positions, it is ironic that administrators viewed Hao's interest in a BGLO fraternity as being in conflict with the other leadership positions he held. The administrators' description of Hao as "mild mannered" and "quiet" also seems at odds with his extensive leadership on campus. It seems more likely that the administrators' response to Hao's BGLO membership reflects assumptions about his race as compared to other BGLO members' race. In line with the reactions Thomas received, Hao's excerpt points to a racialized system whereby Asians and Blacks are distinct racial groups with little expectation for cross-racial relationships.

Racial Boundary Enforcement: Rightness of Whiteness

Similar to the boundary enforcement experienced by non-Black members in the previous section, white members also described how their membership brought attention to their assumed place in the racial hierarchy, particularly, in this case, from family members. Although some of our white respondents described being raised to hold more liberal racial attitudes, they learned that there was a limit to those teachings. BGLO membership was seen by some as taking those principles a step too far. Amber, a 31-year-old white sorority member at a large public university, explained:

> My parents, they taught me when I was young to love everybody and not to be racist and not to discriminate. I would say as I was joining [sorority], going through that whole process, they weren't particularly fond of me joining a predominantly Black organization or surrounding myself with Black people, as they would've defined it. So, while my parents aren't racist, they weren't necessarily fond of me, you know, I guess they felt like I was going too far in the other direction.

For Amber's parents, holding non-discriminatory racial attitudes was an important lesson but having actual relationships with Black people was unnecessary, and, in fact, unwanted. There was a distinct limit to the friendships and associations Amber was to have.

Samantha, a 22-year-old white sorority member at a medium-sized private university, experienced a similar reaction to her BGLO membership from family members. She shared: "They [mom and grandmother] always told me, especially when I went through [sorority], they were like, 'You are choosing a harder life for yourself. Why would you do this?'" In essence, Samantha's mother and grandmother were inquiring why she would give up her white privilege and associate herself with Black people. Interestingly, embedded in this assumption is that associating with Black individuals could somehow compromise Samantha's own life opportunities and her ability to exercise white privilege. Questions like these from whites, insinuations of being not quite white, and mistreatment because of her BGLO affiliation (which we turn to in the next section) were all part of "choosing a harder life."

For Justin, 22-year-old white fraternity member at a large private university, his father eventually accepted his BGLO membership but only after his racial biases were disproven. Justin explained:

> My dad's side of the family are all white Greeks. They were accepting but they definitely didn't understand and were uncomfortable with the concept. It wasn't until my dad came down to [my university] and met some of my fraternity brothers and realized like, "Wow, these guys are just as intelligent as my son if not more intelligent. They're good people." It really took him a while to warm up to the idea. But once he realized I was happy and the people I was surrounding myself with were good people and they would help me, he was able to come to terms with that.

Justin's BGLO membership was an unexpected departure from family norms. The expectation was that if he joined a fraternity it would be a white Greek-letter organization. Further, Justin's characterization of his father's acceptance illustrates the racist belief that Black people are generally inferior and specifically less intelligent than whites. Where the division between whites and Blacks was implicit in Amber's and Samantha's families' responses, Justin's excerpt explicitly illustrates some whites' belief in the superiority of whiteness.

Racial Boundary Enforcement: Not Quite White

White respondents also experienced boundary enforcement from other whites as well as non-whites, who expressed surprise, ambivalence, and disapproval about their decision. In short, these responses indicated that these white BGLO members were acting outside the expectations for their racial group and by doing so were relinquishing some of their whiteness. Samantha, the white sorority member, explained:

> There's always like an ongoing joke [among her white women friends at school] like, "Oh yeah if I was Black, I'd go Delta." Or "If I was Black, I'd go AKA [Alpha Kappa Alpha] …" And it always made me feel like a little offended, like well, why do you have to be Black? Does it make me not white?

Amber, the white sorority member, recalled the questions about her racial identity and BGLO membership, stating:

I think that it was kind of an assumption that like, if this white girl on a campus of mostly white people is joining a Black organization, she must have something, she must be mixed with something, she must have, you know, something else going on.

Similarly, Chris, a 22-year-old white fraternity member at a large public university, recounted:

I've seen that people have looked at me differently when they did know what my letters meant. I mean I've been walking through a department store with my letters on before and I had some guy randomly just look at me and say, "[Fraternity name], really? Why would you do that?" Like I mean, I've had people, like when I'm downtown say things like that, or people tell [me] why would I betray my culture?

As Samantha's, Amber's, and Chris's experiences show, BGLO membership was seen as an affront to white participants' whiteness by other white individuals. For white BGLO members, their membership marked them as racial or cultural outsiders, putting them squarely on the "non-white" side of the white/non-white racial divide. Samantha and Chris's boundary crossing also challenges the construction of white identity. Whiteness is often created in contrast to Blackness. As these individuals chose to align themselves with Blackness by pledging membership to a Black organization, then the basis of their white identities is lost.

In addition to critiques from co-ethnics, friends, strangers, and campus administrators outside BGLOs, respondents also relayed instances of boundary enforcement from BGLO members, which ranged from subtle displeasure to outright rejection of the respondent as an equal and full member. For example, Kelly, a 42-year-old white sorority member who joined a graduate chapter, spoke about her experiences with sorors outside her immediate BGLO chapter:

I'm wondering who's going to be accepting and who's not. I'm conscious of that. I'm not oblivious. And there are interactions, you can tell … You can just tell by their actions. It's more they're uncomfortable. They're uncomfortable.

Kelly describes her reception as laced with apprehension by members of her organization who may not be familiar with her, highlighting the surprise that BGLO members have that white students would come to associate with and join BGLOs. Though Kelly is quite aware of how uncomfortable some sorors may be with her membership, it is unclear if she is aware of how her comfort in these spaces is related to her whiteness. Though Kelly described at great length during her interview her reasons for membership and her desire to come alongside her sorors to fulfill the mission of their BGLO, others outside her immediate chapter are not familiar with her ideals and beliefs, and this leads them to feel uncomfortable with their presence.

Far from just being surprised or uncomfortable, other respondents shared instances of explicit rejection from other BGLO members. Amber, a 31-year-old white sorority member at a large public university, shared an experience that happened to her as she was joining her sorority:

> This was an old [sorority member], she had graduated a few years before, so she came down to visit, and I had never met her before. And she was really upset that they were letting a white girl into the sorority and she treated me accordingly … She said a lot of really ignorant things; just basically she didn't want white people in her sorority.

Despite her chapter members' acceptance of her as a potential member, Amber was neither welcomed nor wanted by everyone. This older sorority member saw the sorority as an organization for Blacks only, and perceived whiteness as potential threat. As previously described, BGLOs provide a refuge for Black students on racially divided and hostile college campuses. Allowing non-Black individuals, and especially white individuals, into this space brings questions about how their presence may change or alter the organization. In fact, white presence in a Black space, created by and for Black people, may be seen as part of a longer history of white interlopers taking over and redirecting Black initiatives. In this way, fears of intrusion, co-optation, and cultural theft are often part of the ongoing controversy over white BGLO members. On the other hand, this type of cross-racial relationship and bonding may be essential to fulfill some of the missions of BGLO organizations, as they push for enhanced racial justice.

Justin, the white fraternity member, shared how he was also initially not well received by fellow fraternity members. However, over time, members came to accept him. Justin shared: "There are people who originally weren't cool with it, that kinda didn't like the idea of a white brother, who have come to terms with it. The line I get normally is that … 'Oh, he's not white; he's Black. He's just extra, extra light skinned.'"

In comparison to the outright rejection described previously, Justin's experience initially appears to indicate eventual full inclusion. However, the explanation of his acceptance, "He's not white; he's Black. He's just extra, extra light skinned," underscores a similar rigidity around race. In order for some fraternity members to accept him into their Black organization, he must be thought of as not quite white.

Paradoxically, although non-white BGLO members were often viewed as betraying their whiteness by outsiders or described as being honorary Blacks by their BGLO sisters or brothers, BGLO membership for whites also led respondents to increase their acknowledgment and identity as white individuals, as discussed in the previous chapter. Due to the strong white/non-white divide in play in the college campus environment, white BGLO members experience both a strengthening and understanding of their identities as white members of Black organizations, and a sentiment that their BGLO membership sets them apart racially and culturally from other whites, and may even place them on the "non-white" side of the divide.

Racial Boundary Enforcement: "If You're Not Black, You're White To Me"

White BGLO members were not the only participants who experienced the sentiment that BGLOs were for Blacks only. Although the non-Black members of color we spoke to often felt bound together with their Black brothers and sisters by their racial marginality, Black BGLO members and other non-members still viewed these non-Black members as crossing a color-line. Osita, a 33-year-old Latina sorority member who joined a graduate chapter, describes a reaction to her membership, stating:

> I feel like some of the more challenging components have been more passive. I've gone to regional conferences and I've gone to even student affairs conferences and it's a Greek social or things like that, and I wear my letters or I wear my pin, and I think I've gotten some looks of people, that's like, "Uhhh what are you doing here? Who are you?" kind of thing. But I don't think anybody's outright criticized me or come in a negative manner … People were surprised at times.

Osita's experience of other BGLO members being surprised at her membership showcases a Black/non-Black divide. Even though Osita was not white, because she was not Black some felt that she did not quite belong within a Black organization. Osita experienced disapproval through subtle confused looks, but some participants received more explicit messages that they did not belong in a BGLO, even if they were a student of color. For example, Hao, the Vietnamese fraternity member, said, "I actually get more pushback from other fraternity folks. Matter of fact, the first week that I crossed, I remember a member of [my fraternity] came up to me and said, 'F– you, you're not Black. You don't belong in this fraternity.'" Similarly, Bailey, the white-Hispanic sorority member, discusses an experience with her sorority sisters:

> At one point, one of the ladies in my chapter made a joke once, and I mean, I know she was kidding but there's a little truth behind it. Where she was like, "Hey, if you're not Black, you're white to me." And that's what she always used to say, and I really think that's how a lot of people feel. There's Black and there's white and that's it … You're either one of us or you're not. And I do feel like I do get that a lot from Black Greeks.

Although our non-white respondents felt that they did not fit in with whites on their racially divided college campuses and tried to find refuge through BGLO membership, these responses show that not all fellow BGLO members were accepting of their membership. Their membership was still identified as over-stepping a racial boundary, highlighting that a white/non-white racial divide may not fit for all experiences on campus. The distancing from and outright rejection of non-Black members may reflect Black BGLO members' desire to maintain their organizations as a space created by and for Black people. Interactions with outsiders and fellow BGLO members served as reminders that respondents were only a small part of a much larger racial stratification system. However, how they experienced that stratification system varied based on their own race and the particular context of their organization and campus.

Conclusion

The contemporary college or university is not a post-racial or colorblind space. Instead, we find that vestiges of colleges' racist pasts continue to shape contemporary campus racial climates, despite the increasing amount of attention to diversity and inclusivity that administrative rhetoric and admissions websites provide. We found that our respondents repeatedly mentioned how the severe racial divide char-acterized their campus racial climate, which led to increased solidarity across the non-white members of their campus. This finding held true for the majority of respondents, whose college context ranged from small liberal arts colleges to large public universities, showing that smaller or more intimate higher education settings do not necessarily alleviate racial isolation or racial hostility.

In this context, then, we find that BGLOs, which were originally founded in response to the types of racial exclusion that Black Americans experienced on college campuses, continue to serve their purpose as a necessary counter-space, but that also non-Blacks come to identify with these organizations in order to develop meaningful interracial solidarity and to oppose their hostile campus climates. Because of respondents' perception that college campuses lack mean-ingful attention to race, racism, and racial realities, their membership in BGLOs becomes a lived experience of identification with these issues, serving as a pragmatic space where students can engage in meaningful cross-racial interac-tions, foster affective ties, and engage in race-related activism (Hughey and Parks 2011).

Our members' responses demonstrate how the shifting racial landscape plays out on the university campus. For our respondents, entering college served as a key time to understand how they fit within the racial hierarchy at large. Due to jarring racial divides on campus coupled with a lack of compositional racial diversity and curricular inclusion, respondents experienced heightened awareness about themselves and other racial groups, even if race had not been an important or salient factor in their lives previous to college. BGLO membership served as a mechanism for our respondents to resolve this dissonance, wherein students from various racial backgrounds, despite assumptions that they may have separate interests or spaces on campus, felt drawn together under a sense of linked fate (Dawson 1994).

However, once they became a member of these BGLOs, how our participants understood racial stratification became more complicated. Whereas some participants experienced reactions that highlighted how Blackness was distinct and separate from other non-white racial groups, other participants, especially our white respondents, experienced reactions that further solidified their understanding of a white/non-white racial divide. This demonstrates that the racial landscape may be multi-faceted, with several binaries or divides operating at the same time within the same space, such as the college campus. While understanding their place within the racialized landscape was one outcome of their BGLO membership, in the next chapter, we turn to other outcomes from membership.

References

Antonio, Anthony L. 2004. "When Does Race Matter in College Friendships? Exploring Men's Diverse and Homogeneous Friendship Groups." *Review of Higher Education* 27(4):553–575.

Bonilla-Silva, Eduardo. 2004. "From Bi-Racial to Tri-Racial: Towards a New System of Racial Stratification in the USA." *Ethnic & Racial Studies* 27(6):931–950.

Bowman, Nicholas A. 2010. "College Diversity Experiences and Cognitive Development: A Meta-Analysis." *Review of Educational Research* 80(1):4–33.

Bowman, Nicholas A. 2011. "Promoting Participation in a Diverse Democracy: A Meta-Analysis of College Diversity Experiences and Civic Engagement." *Review of Educational Research* 81(1):29–68.

Chang, Mitchell J., Alexander W. Astin, and Dongbin Kim. 2004. "Cross-Racial Interaction among Undergraduates: Some Consequences, Causes, and Patterns." *Research in Higher Education* 45(5):529–553.

Chavous, Tabbye M. 2005. "An Intergroup Contact-Theory Framework for Evaluating Racial Climate on Predominantly White College Campuses." *American Journal of Community Psychology* 36(3/4):239–257.

Chutuape, Erica D. 2016. "'Chinese-Mexicans' and 'Blackest Asians': Filipino American Youth Resisting the Racial Binary." *Race, Ethnicity, and Education* 19(1):200–231.

Dawson, Michael C. 1994. *Behind the Mule: Race and Class in African-American Politics.* Princeton, NJ: Princeton University Press.

Gallagher, Charles A. 1995. "White Reconstruction in the University." *Socialist Review* 94(1&2):165–187.

Gallagher, Charles A. 2004. "Racial Redistricting: Expanding the Boundaries of Whiteness." Pp. 59–76 in *The Politics of Multiracialism*, edited by H.M. Dalmage. New York City: State University of New York Press.

Grasmuck, Sherri and Jennifer Kim. 2010. "Embracing and Resisting Ethnoracial Boundaries: Second-Generation Immigrant and African-American Students in a Multicultural University." *Sociological Forum* 25(2):221–247.

Griggs, Brandon. 2015. "Do U.S. Colleges Have a Race Problem?" CNN.com. Retrieved from www.cnn.com/2015/11/10/us/racism-college-campuses-protests-missouri/ (January 23, 2016).

Gurin, Patricia, Eric Dey, Sylvia Hurtado, and Gerald Gurin. 2002. "Diversity and Higher Education: Theory and Impact on Educational Outcomes." *Harvard Education Review* 72(3):330–367.

Hall, Wendell D., Alberto F. Cabrera, and Jeffrey F. Milem. 2011. "A Tale of Two Groups: Differences between Minority Students and Non-Minority Students in Their Predispositions to and Engagement with Diverse Peers at a Predominantly White Insitution." *Research in Higher Education* 52(4):420–439.

Harper, Shaun R. and Sylvia Hurtado. 2007. "Nine Themes in Campus Racial Climates and Implications for Institutional Transformation." *New Directions for Student Services* 120:7–24.

Harper, Shaun R. and Stephen John Quaye. 2007. "Student Organizations as Venues for Black Identity Expression and Development among African American Male Student Leaders." *Journal of College Student Development* 48(2):127–144.

Hughey, Matthew W. 2010. "A Paradox of Participation: Nonwhites in White Sororities and Fraternities." *Social Problems* 57(4):653–679.

Hughey, Matthew W. and Gregory S. Parks (eds.). 2011. *Black Greek-Letter Organizations 2.0: New Directions in the Study of African American Fraternities and Sororities*. Jackson, MS: University Press of Mississippi.

Hurtado, Sylvia. 2005. "The Next Generation of Diversity and Intergroup Relations Research." *Journal of Social Issues* 61:595–610.

Hurtado, Sylvia, Alma R. Clayton-Pedersen, Walter Recharde Allen, and Jeffrey F. Milem. 1998. "Enhancing Campus Climates for Racial/Ethnic Diversity: Educational Policy and Practice." *Review of Higher Education* 21(3):279–302.

Hurtado, Sylvia and Adriana Ruiz. 2012. "The Climate for Underrepresented Groups and Diversity on Campus." *Higher Education Research Institute at UCLA*.

Hurtado, Sylvia, Adriana Ruiz Alvarado, and Chelsea Guillermo-Wann. 2015. "Thinking about Race: The Salience of Racial Identity at Two- and Four-Year Colleges and the Climate for Diversity." *The Journal of Higher Education* 86(1):127–152.

Inkelas, Karen K. 2004. "Does Participation in Ethnic Co-Curricular Activities Facilitate a Sense of Ethnic Awareness and Understanding? A Study of Asian Pacific American Undergraduates." *Journal of College Student Development* 45(3):285–302.

Kaufmann, Karen M. 2003. "Cracks in the Rainbow: Group Commonality as a Basis for Latino and African-American Political Coalitions." *Political Research Quarterly* 56(2):199–210.

Kim, Claire Jean. 1999. "The Racial Triangulation of Asian Americans." *Politics & Society* 27(1):105–138.

Lee, Jennifer, and Frank D. Bean. 2004. "America's Changing Color Lines: Immigration, Race/Ethnicity, and Multiracial Identification." *Annual Review of Sociology* 30:221–242.

McCabe, Janice. 2011. "Doing Multiculturalism: An Interactionist Analysis of the Practices of a Multicultural Sorority." *Journal of Contemporary Ethnography* 40(5):521–549.

McClain, Paula D., Niambi M. Carter, Victoria M. Defrancesco Soto, Monique L. Lyle, Jeffrey D. Grynaviski, Shayla C. Nunnally, Thomas J. Scotto, J. Alan Kendrick, Gerald F. Lackey, and Kendra D. Cotton. 2006. "Racial Distancing in a Southern City: Latino Immigrants' Views of Black Americans." *Journal of Politics* 68(3):571–584.

Milem, Jeffrey F., Mitchell J. Chang, and Anthony L. Antonio. 2005. *Making Diversity Work on Campus: A Research Based Perspective*. Washington, DC: American Association of Colleges and Universities.

Milem, Jeffrey F. and Kenji Hakuta. 2000. "The Benefits of Racial and Ethnic Diversity in Higher Education." Pp. 39–67 in *Minorities in Higher Education, 1999–2000, Seventeenth Annual Status Report*, edited by D.J. Wilds. Washington, DC: American Council on Education.

Museus, Samuel D. 2008. The Role of Ethnic Student Organizations in Fostering African American and Asian American Students' Cultural Adjustment and Membership at Predominantly White Institutions." *Journal of College Student Development* 46(6):568–586.

Patton, Tracey Owens. 2008. "Jim Crow on Fraternity Row: A Study of the Phenomenon of Blackface in the White Southern Fraternal Order." *Visual Communication Quarterly* 15(3):150–168.

Ross, Lawrence. 2016. *Blackballed: The Black and White Politics of Race on America's Campuses.* New York, NY: St. Martin's Press.

Shiao, Jiannbin Lee, and Mia H. Tuan. 2008. "Korean Adoptees and the Social Context of Ethnic Exploration." *American Journal of Sociology* 113(4):1023–1066.

Solorzano, Daniel, Miguel Ceja, and Tara Yosso. 2000. "Critical Race Theory, Racial Microaggressions, and Campus Racial Climate: The Experiences of African American College Students." *Journal of Negro Education* 69(1):60–73.

Ward, Kelly Marie, and Maria Estela Zarate. 2015. "The Influence of Campus Racial Climate on Graduate Student Attitudes about the Benefits of Diversity." *The Review of Higher Education* 38(4):589–617.

Warikoo, Natasha K., and Sherry L. Deckman. 2014. "Beyond the Numbers: Institutional Influences on Experiences with Diversity on Elite College Campuses." *Sociological Forum* 29(4):959–981.

Warren, Jonathan W., and France Winddance Twine. 1997. "White Americans, The New Majority?: Non-Blacks and the Ever-Expanding Boundaries of Whiteness." *The Journal of Black Studies* 28(2):200–218.

Yancey, George. 2003. *Who is White? Latinos, Asians, and the New Black/NonBlack Divide.* Boulder, CO: Lynne Rienner Publishers.

4

BRANDED FOR LIFE

The Impact of Membership

> Like from the day one, when I went to rush to see what it was about to the day
> when I had my new initiate presentation, I was a completely different woman.
> *Samantha, 22-year-old white sorority member*

The initiation of a new pledge class or 'line' into a Black Greek-letter organization's (BGLO) chapter is often an exciting and suspense-filled time on campus. Who has made the line is often kept secret, only revealed to the campus during a probate show or new initiate presentation. Traditionally the term 'probates' referred to pledges, or people undergoing initiation into the organization (Kimbrough 2003). The probate performance or 'show' happened preceding formal initiation into the organization (Kimbrough 2003). However, with the change from extensive pledging prior to official membership to a truncated membership intake process after admission in the 1990s, probate shows often occur after new members have officially joined the organization.

During a probate show, the newly inducted chapter members recite organizational history and chants, often through call and response, step or stroll, and are presented to the campus community and graduate members as official members of the organization. Former chapter members often travel far and wide to see the probate. These very public performances serve multiple purposes. The preparation to put on a step show requires dedication, physical stamina, and teamwork, which continue a sense of community and bonding among new members that began with their initiation. Moreover, at a very basic level, the probate serves as a presentation of new members to the chapter and campus community. The performance of the new members demonstrates that the chapter has made a wise decision in selecting these new members and that they will uphold the traditions and knowledge of the organization.

Finally, through the probate, performers express a connection to African American cultural traditions. Drawing on both historic and contemporary dance and musical traditions, the probate serves as a continuation of traditions from the past as well as a site of innovation, an element fundamental to African American cultural forms. In *Soulstepping: African American Step Shows*, Elizabeth C. Fine examines the cultural and historic roots of BGLO stepping. She states:

> As an oral tradition, stepping gains flexibility through the use of a wide variety of other traditional expressive forms and patterns such as call and response, rapping, the dozens, signifying, marking, spirituals, handclap games, and military chants. In addition, stepping movements, songs, and chants borrow from a long history of African American traditions, some deriving from slave and minstrel dances and others from such popular influences as tap, the lindy hop, the Florida A&M University band, black cheerleading, break dancing and hip-hop, military marching, and New Orleans street parades.
>
> *(Fine 2003:70)*

In detailing the connections to various musical forms and dance styles, Fine argues for the role of probates as a ritual marking a rite of passage from uninitiated to initiated BGLO member. As such, at a community level, the probate also serves as a bonding ritual among the new and old members. Through chants, calls, and recitation of organizational history, performers verbally announce their group affiliation while also bolstering in-group status for both performers and audience members who are fellow organization members. Simultaneously, this performance asserts the organization's superiority, bolstering its attractiveness for potential members and in contrast to other BGLOs. The boundary demarcations of probate shows – between new initiates and non-members; between members, both new and old; and other BGLOs' members – also extend to the larger campus community. Probate shows, while particular to the specific organization welcoming a new line, serve as a community-building event among the Black Greek-letter community and Black student population at large.

The shared group identity as members of a specific BGLO showcased in the probate is key to fostering the lifelong bonds of brotherhood and sisterhood characterizing Black fraternities and sororities. These organizations were originally conceived of as vehicles for developing Black leadership and racial uplift, through sustained relationships between members, old and new. As we reveal in this chapter, these elements also extend to non-Black members. Specifically, our participants felt that the skills that they learned in BGLOs carried over to impact their self-esteem and self-confidence, leadership and workplace aptitudes, and career choices. Moreover, the non-Black members we spoke with cited additional effects of their BGLO membership explaining how their BGLO membership also affected their relationships with their family, particularly around ideas of race and racism.

Building Boldness: Self-confidence and Speaking Out

Given the public and performative nature of probate shows, it is unsurprising that Samantha, whose words opened this chapter, identifies participation in it as key to building her self-confidence. She explained in more detail the importance of her probate or new initiate presentation to her self-esteem:

> I'm a lot more confident when I speak ... That's definitely one of the biggest aspects it's helped me with is become more confident in what I have to say. I've also been told that since I did cross into [my sorority], people are like, "Yeah, you already had a presence on campus but just like the way you carry yourself. You're more proud. You are more confident in things you do." And it was really good because, I, before I even pledged [my sorority], I already created an organization [focused on LGBTQ inclusivity], but even after that I've just took on so many more leader roles. And I just felt I had more impact in the community and I felt like I had more of a voice. So it gave me more confidence in myself that I didn't already see I had.

Samantha's self-confidence, including her outspokenness and her leadership capabilities, increased as a result of pledging her BGLO. Even though she created an LGBTQ inclusivity organization prior to joining her sorority, which speaks to her leadership capabilities, after she crossed she felt more confident in taking on additional leadership positions. When we asked her what aided in developing this confidence, Samantha responded: "Through my sisters ... just them talking to me and being there for me and just experiencing my process with my sisters ... going through just the process and having my new initiate presentation."

Samantha's believes that her pledge process and the bonding therein with her line sisters fostered her confidence. Likewise, her line's new initiate presentation provided a platform for her to showcase the 'new woman' she had become while also continuing to build her self-esteem. Similarly, Chris, a 22-year-old white fraternity member, shared, "I used to be shy before I joined my organization and now it's definitely brought me out more." He explained how his membership made him more extroverted and confident:

> I feel like when you do a Greek-letter, a Black Greek-letter organization, they have certain things that kind of make you to be more prominent on campus. You have to probate for one, which is, it's stressful in the beginning ... Then you have step shows, and you have stroll offs. Just the process of that and getting to know everybody in the Black community on [my university's] campus.

It is telling that in addition to public performances like his probate, step shows, and stroll offs that Chris mentions "getting to know everybody in the Black community" on campus as developing his self-confidence. This underscores the tight-knit nature of the Black community on predominantly white campuses, as many respondents noted in the previous chapter. However, this may also point to both Chris's previous unfamiliarity with and outsider status among the school's Black community, as well as his hyper-visibility as a non-Black BGLO member.

Due to the normative institutional arrangements on predominantly white campuses that structure campus life, such as financial resources and campus notoriety, Black and white Greek life is segregated (Ray 2013). For example, Black and white fraternities and sororities are often spatially separated, with white fraternities and sororities having organizational houses and Black Greek organizations instead being housed in an office in the student union or cultural center (Ray 2013). Demographically, the Black student population is numerically much smaller than the white student population at predominantly white campuses. Accordingly, BGLO chapters comprise far fewer members than the average white Greek organization. Often, white students are not even aware of BGLOs.

This smaller and close-knit nature of the Black student community leads to the hyper-visibility of BGLO members in general. For example, whereas a white Greek-letter member may be able to blend in with the large white student population, a Black Greek-letter member would most likely be known and noted within the Black student population regardless of if she were wearing Greek-letter paraphernalia. Given that non-Black BGLO members are the exception rather than the norm, they may experience acute hyper-visibility, particularly among the Black student population. Quyen, a 31-year-old Vietnamese fraternity member, expands upon this idea of hyper-visibility as a non-Black member of a BGLO and its effects on his level of extroversion:

> I would definitely say, it made me more outgoing … I was very reserved before and being that I'm an Asian person hanging around a lot of Black people, I just kinda sat there and kinda just I really didn't try to get to know people. [My fraternity] really opened that up to me. We, I, traveled a lot with my chapter. Even on campus I got to know a lot of people in white fraternities and athletes and just people in general just because they kinda know who you are and you stand out, really stand out. And so that definitely helped me in that aspect.

Quyen first explains how his racial identity as an Asian person among Black peers made him feel inhibited. These reservations raise concerns regarding if Quyen felt his acceptance among his Black brothers was conditional – was he unable to fully fraternize with his brothers due to external cues or internal policing? He obviously felt some level of comfort and acceptance with his Black peers in order to "[hang] around a lot of Black people" and pledge a Black organization, yet despite this, he was "very reserved." However, through his BGLO membership he had more opportunities to meet people and was expected to be more outgoing. Whether it was through traveling with his chapter members or his position as a non-Black BGLO member, Quyen had a responsibility to represent his organization. In these instances, he was expected to get to know people and in doing so he became more extroverted.

While Quyen's racial difference from his fraternity brothers and the accountability to his organization fostered a more outgoing personality, Michael, a 22-year-old white fraternity member, shared how this racial difference from his fraternity brothers led him to a different mindset:

> But, I think the best, the main thing that it has done for me is really given me that sense of community while also motivating me to continue to want to branch out myself, and it's made me a lot more comfortable with being uncomfortable. And, what I mean by that is, greater than race, but it kinda starts there. Like going to a convention, for instance, and I'm one of the ten white people in thousands of guys. There are times where I feel like all eyes might be on me, but at the same it's made me comfortable with that and realizing that I am and I can be comfortable with being this person and being uncomfortable in a given situation.

Michael's BGLO membership serves as a foundation for making new connections or undertaking projects that may be outside his comfort zone. In a typically unusual form of tokenism, Michael points out that at fraternity conventions he is often one of very few white people among thousands of Black men. Though Michael uses this experience to bolster his confidence and work through being uncomfortable due racial hyper-visibility, we are careful not to generalize the resolution he reaches to the experiences of other individuals. Here, whether he makes the connection or not, Michael experiences the type of racial hyper-visibility during this once-a-year conference that his fraternity brothers likely face daily outside the fraternity. Whereas Michael can retreat to the normalcy of whiteness, his Black fraternity brothers remain racially othered within society writ large. In giving the example of attending a fraternity convention, Michael underscores the different experiences non-Black members have when they're among BGLO members outside their chapter or local area. Respondents generally felt accepted by their chapter members; however, they often felt members encountered at regional or national meetings were less accepting, as we discussed in the previous chapter. Michael identifies feeling highly visible and scrutinized but instead of feeling ostracized, those experiences bolster his confidence as a white man in a Black fraternity.

Similarly, Hao, a 35-year-old Vietnamese man, echoes this idea of confidence and pushing through internal boundaries, stating:

> It's pushed me into a direction of not being complacent and being, always thinking progressively … it's pushed me to think differently. It's pushed me

to approach things differently. I don't look at things in too much of a negative light anymore. I always look at how can we all adjust or improve or get better. That's always my mindset at this point. So, it's definitely changed my life.

Hao's membership shaped his mindset to focus on community solutions. Instead of being complacent with current conditions, he now thinks about how he can contribute to solutions for improving the circumstances of those around him. Similarly, Jessica, a 22-year-old white sorority member, referred to a confidence in speaking up for injustice, explaining:

I'm an outgoing person but it's made me, I guess, more willing to speak out. Just because sometimes I'm like, "Oh, I don't know what people will say if I express myself in this way." But like yesterday our university actually organized a silent protest for Baltimore and for some things that are happening on our campus. And two of my line sisters were two of the big organizers behind that and I helped as well, helped set up everything, and talked to some news reporters and stuff. And I was thinking about it, and I was like, I don't think I would have been brave enough to have done that and to have reached out to people and tried to get people involved and all that kind of stuff and helped organize it if it weren't for [my sorority]. And, I feel like it's just made me a lot braver in myself, a lot more confident in myself. It's kind of raised my self-esteem, and I think that's due to our beliefs and due to the people surrounding me as well, because they're kind of like, "You can do whatever you put your mind to."

Here Jessica references a silent protest for Baltimore in response to the death of Freddie Gray, Jr. while in police custody. On April 12, 2015 Baltimore police arrested Gray, who sustained neck and spinal injuries when transported in a police vehicle (Graham 2015). He remained comatose in the hospital until his death a week later. His death was among many high-profile, excessive police force incidents and spurred a series of protests and civil unrest in Baltimore. Cities across the U.S. demonstrated in solidarity. Jessica's excerpt highlights how her membership in her Black sorority increased her confidence in speaking out, in general, and against racial injustice in particular. As a result of her increased confidence and self-esteem coupled with her organization's racial justice initiatives and being in the company of her sorority sisters, Jessica feels emboldened to advocate for justice.

Jessica's experience also alludes to the racialized expectations that dissuade participation in racial justice organizing. Even though Jessica describes herself as outgoing, she has doubts regarding her involvement in racial justice activism due to the fear of criticism. Any backlash she faces is likely rooted in the idea that as a white woman, Jessica is acting outside the norms of racial expectations. Research finds that among white college students reflections on whiteness, power, and privilege are necessary for racial justice ally development (Reason et al. 2005). Introspection alone, however, is not sufficient. Without high-quality interracial interactions, meaningful engagement with racial diversity does not occur. Additionally, researchers find that white students often feel they need an invitation to engage in racial justice work and do not proactively get involved. For other students, their involvement with student organizations provides the opportunity and responsibility to engage in racial justice work. Jessica's reflection on her internal policing demonstrates a barrier to racial justice work among whites. However, her BGLO membership provided the chance to engage in this type of work while also providing ongoing high-quality interracial interactions. Alessandra, a 44-year-old Guatemalan sorority member, also discussed how her BGLO membership increased her confidence in speaking out and organizing:

> I have a stronger voice when it comes to certain things that I can stand behind something … It has kind of helped me to realize that in all things we are responsible to answer to. So there's a lot of accountability. There's a lot of accountability as a result of being a member of this organization because of the types of involvement and the things that I am involved in even on things that are unrelated to the sorority – my civic duties and my community responsibilities outside of the sorority. My involvement with my sorority really helps to shape those things because it helps me to see what gaps, where my services could best be used, and what gaps there are in order for me to be a better servant to my community.

For Alessandra, service through her sorority is only a starting point for her commitment to community uplift. Through her sorority membership, Alessandra feels an immense responsibility to her community and a confidence in her ability to stand for her beliefs. On a deeper level, Alessandra is referring to a change in her orientation to the world and the accountability that stems from this understanding. Similar to the shift in perspective that Hao mentioned, Alessandra is articulating an accountability not only to her sorority and community at large but rather to the type of person she has become through her community engagement. For her, she must live these ideals in all aspects of her life.

However, Charisse, a 23-year-old Filipina sorority member, reminds us that membership in and of itself does not lead to positive outcomes, but rather it is the commitment to action supporting the ideals of the organization. She explains:

> It's not the letters you're wearing. It's pretty much how you make your letters at the end of the day. How do you make a mark in [the sorority]. I feel like I represent the scholarship; I know I have the service and, of course, sisterhood is already impacted within that already. So it's just more of the idea that the accomplishments that I've had in [my sorority] that's given me that confidence. I'm going out in a community and doing all of this community

service, and I've helped many people, many young girls, helped educate [them] about college life. It makes you feel good about yourself … I'm helping make change.

Charisse's excerpt exemplifies the popular saying among BGLO members of "you make the letters, the letters don't make you." In other words, each BGLO member has the responsibility to uphold the standards of their organization and give the organization its meaning. Simply being a member does not transform an individual into someone else. Through living up to the ideals of her sorority, Charisse's feels that her self-confidence has increased. In particular, because of her community service, including mentoring young girls specifically, she feels a connection to the community and part of positively impacting the next generation of young women. She identifies her efforts in community engagement increase her well-being. In fact, research finds that volunteer work enhances multiple aspects of personal well-being including levels of happiness, self-esteem, and self-mastery (Wilson 2000). These positive outcomes are facilitated by the general sense of feeling that one matters or one is needed, and increases in empathy (Borgonovi 2008). BGLO membership and the service commitment provide respondents with meaning and purpose. Research finds that volunteer work in and of itself is only one component that leads to increased well-being; the conditions surrounding the volunteer work also increase self-esteem and self-mastery (Thoits and Hewitt 2001). For example, volunteers are more likely to experience positive outcomes if the work provides an opportunity for self-direction and autonomy or if the work is challenging. BGLO service may be particularly applicable to these conditions. While service is nationally mandated, it is developed and implemented through the chapter level. Therefore, chapter members have a high level of autonomy in enacting and shaping service within their home communities.

On the Shoulders of Giants: The Legacy and Responsibility of Leadership

In pledging BGLOs, respondents were joining a long history of leadership, service, and racial justice activism. Individual BGLO members and BGLOs as a collective entity were instrumental in securing civil rights (Hernandez and Parks 2016; Laybourn and Parks 2016a, 2016b, 2016c; Parks and Neumann 2015; Parks et al. 2014). Throughout the early decades of their founding, BGLOs engaged in letter-writing campaigns and lobbying, partnerships with other justice organizations, and litigation to advance the cause of civil rights. In the late 1940s, six BGLOs established the American Council on Human Rights (ACHR) to pressure the federal government to enact civil rights policies (American Council on Human Rights, Commission on Evaluation 1954). ACHR was an expansion of Alpha Kappa Alpha Sorority, Incorporated's National Non-Partisan Council of Public Affairs (NPCPA). NPCPA's goals were to improve conditions for African

Americans in the sectors of education, employment, and public service. Similarly, ACHR's goals were to ensure civil rights for all Americans regardless of race or religion.

The non-Black BGLO members that we spoke to often called upon this legacy of civil rights activism in explaining why they joined their respective organization. Roano, a 38-year-old Puerto Rican fraternity member, explained:

> It is a beautiful history in this country related to how our organization has been involved politically and socially in the advancement of civil rights in this country from our iconic members who are, our most famous members, whether it is Thurgood Marshall or Martin Luther King [Jr.]. Our members definitely take pride in the role the fraternity has played. And that's a huge humbling piece when we become members to know that our story is now tied to theirs. We are because they were here.

Roano calls upon the history of his fraternity to explain the responsibility of having his organization tied to a legacy of greatness. Similarly, Sofia, a 27-year-old white-Hispanic sorority member, explained:

> Once I started doing research on, really doing research on Delta, just the story of the Founders, how they participated in the Women's Suffrage March [in 1913],[1] and how they were the only Black women's organization there. And, they had to have a chaperone. They were told not to come. They went anyways. They stepped out on faith. Then I learned a lot of my role models, because my degree is in African American studies, were Deltas. You know, Mary McLeod Bethune,[2] Shirley Chisholm,[3] Barbara Jordan.[4] I was like, "There is something special about these women. I want to be a part of that." Those were my role models.

As with other respondents, Sofia felt a connection to her particular organization's history of activism, as well as individual influential members. By pledging their BGLO, members tapped into an important legacy but also cultivated those characteristics within themselves. Sofia went on to explain how several women who were influential in her early undergraduate years, were also Deltas, including her residential coordinator and her work studies director. For example:

> My freshman year in college, I remember, her name's Ms. DeAndrea. She was walking across campus … when I saw Ms. DeAndrea and I saw the way, just the way she carried herself. Her head was up and she had a briefcase at her side. And I said, "Something is special about that woman." She ended up being my residential coordinator, and she played no games. She had very high standards.

Other respondents also made the connection to their organization's historic well-known leaders, as well as student leaders on their campus who were members of their organization. Thomas, a 26-year-old Vietnamese-Filipino fraternity member, stated:

> My goals for undergrad, which was all leadership and service, I noticed a lot of people who were all part of the same organization, were prominent leaders, activists, civically engaged folks around my university and they were all part of my fraternity. That kind of was a starting point for me. Eventually I did my own research and saw a lot of names that appear in many books and really was enamored by a legacy that I think meant so much more in a community that I would be really proud to be a part of.

Todd, a 20-year-old Mexican-Japanese man, echoes his point, stating:

> I saw more in Alpha Phi Alpha that I felt I was more suited [to] and fit me better than the other organizations. Not to mention, the people that were part of Alpha Phi Alpha on campus and people throughout history, like Martin Luther King [Jr.] and W.E.B. Du Bois and Lionel Richie. That really caught my eye. Also, the students on campus that were part of Alpha Phi Alpha were also some of my friends that were in gospel choir with me. And they were just strong men in Christ as well as just strong students on campus, so it really inspired me to join Alpha Phi Alpha over the other organizations.

Taken together, the experiences of Sofia, Thomas, and Todd indicate a need for positive role models and social support networks. It is not only that membership allowed our respondents to join an important history but also that through membership, respondents saw positive renderings of people of color. Their membership was also a way to affirm their own identity and place on their college campus and society at large.

Leadership and service were already often part of our respondents' undergraduate experience, but they saw a way to make those commitments more meaningful through their BGLO membership. Thomas and Todd also indicate that their respective chapter members were people who were involved throughout campus organizations, not only their fraternity. This mirrors research that finds BGLO members are more likely to be members of other student organizations compared to non-Greeks, and that BGLO members hold more elected leadership positions than non-Greeks (Erwin et al. 2004; Kimbrough and Hutcheson 1998). Research also finds BGLO members feel more confident in their leadership abilities than non-Greeks (Kimbrough and Hutcheson 1998). This may be in part because BGLOs provide more opportunities for leadership development and enactment of leadership skills (Sutton and Terrell 1997). As such, BGLO members report thinking of themselves as leaders regardless of if they hold an elected leadership position and that they conceptualize community service as a form of leadership, differing from perspectives outside BGLOs (Kimbrough 1995; Sutton and Kimbrough 2001).

Todd also explained the responsibility he felt to continue the legacy of the great men who came before him in his fraternity:

> I feel like every Alpha man or every person who's joined Alpha Phi Alpha Fraternity, Incorporated has just done great things or is in great things, and I feel it's my role to also help out and do whatever I can to also do great things. There's a quote that Alpha Phi Alpha uses, and it's "The work of Alpha is never done." And it's all about what you can do for Alpha rather than what Alpha can do for you … I'm going to do my best to see what I can do for Alpha and by doing that come up with inventive ways to help out the community in any way possible.

This idea of going beyond solely being part of a legacy of great individuals by pledging a Black Greek organization to bearing a responsibility to continue that legacy was echoed by other respondents. For example, Adam, a 39-year-old white fraternity member, explained:

> For me, it essentially came down to the founding principles, right. White Greek organizations were historically organizations to maintain, set up to maintain the status quo, whereas Black Greek-letter organizations were initiated as agents of change. Every Black Greek-letter organization that was founded, was founded under pretty revolutionary principles. I mean we can go back to Alpha Phi Alpha at Cornell, these were guys that were trying to change the world, and trying to change the status quo and challenge the status quo and then that rang true with me … This goes with all Black Greek-letter organizations, I've seen it across the board, but my experience was in personally witnessing the members of [my fraternity] and how they were dedicated to helping the community, and I was like, "I want to be a part of that."

Adam draws out an important difference between historically white and historically Black Greek organizations. Unlike white organizations, BGLOs have a racial justice focus that requires a lifelong commitment. This significant difference emphasizes why non-Black members are often viewed with suspicion, as members might question the longevity of their commitment and their authenticity in agreeing with the mission of the organization. However, this distinguishing feature also may explain why some non-Black members choose to align themselves with BGLOs. In Adam's case, his membership allowed him to ally himself with racial justice.

Black fraternities and sororities have a long legacy of leadership, social justice activism, and community uplift. As these members' experiences highlight, joining

this history of great leaders and continuing that legacy in the fight towards social justice is one reason respondents joined their respective organizations. While overall BGLOs share a focus on scholarship, leadership, and service, each BGLO has unique nationally mandated programs that are focused on different aspects of racial uplift (for more detailed information about BGLO programming, see Chapter 1).

Each BGLO has a national agenda for service, but it is the chapters that implement those service initiatives in their local communities. As such, chapter members are responsible for organizing and planning their community service programs as well as any other chapter-sponsored events. Events include voter registration drives, health screenings, after-school tutoring for young children, environmental sustainability initiatives, financial literacy workshops, and fundraising events. Through developing, planning, and organizing events like these, respondents gained hands-on leadership skills. These skills facilitated their professional development and often translated into marketable job skills. Bailey, a 24-year-old white-Hispanic sorority member, explains:

> [BGLO membership] has taught me so much from just being a team player and learning how to really run things with a team to really teaching me how to run a business. When you're in undergrad and you have, like I said, we suffered having a very small chapter for many years, so when you have four or five people trying to run a business and run a chapter and do all the things that involves, you really learn a lot about ownership and accountability. And those are things I have absolutely taken into my professional life and my adult life.

Unlike white Greek organizations, which frequently have upwards of a hundred members, BGLOs have a much smaller pool of potential members. As such, the chapters are typically less in number, and at times, even only in the single digits. Bailey's comment alludes to one particular aspect of these small enrollment numbers. Regardless of how many members there are in a particular chapter, they are still responsible for meeting the nationally mandated service projects. Thus, a smaller chapter size means that more onus is on each individual member to actively implement the service components. Although this responsibility could be overwhelming to members, Bailey recounts her experience in her chapter positively, stating that it helped her learn how to "run a business" which has benefited her in her professional life. Interestingly, Khashifa, a 35-year-old Pakistani sorority member, also makes the analogy of running a chapter to running a business. In her case, she was a member of the charter line of her school's chapter, or initial pledge class of a new nationally approved chapter.

> Starting a chapter from scratch you learn, it was basically like running a business on campus … By the time we got our chapter and everything, we

were like 20. So at 20 years old, trying to run a business from beginning to end. We had to raise money. We had nationals that we had to satisfy. We had our graduate chapter, so like you could say those were our bosses, right … And then let's say, our competitors, like [other National Pan-Hellenic Council sororities] and dealing with the competing organizations, creating alliances. It's like a total business from beginning to end, shaping the culture on campus. I mean we came in and we changed the entire face of campus … We totally introduced a whole new way of life on campus. We did extensive programming for the Black community on campus. There was no fun programming on campus geared toward minority students … I mean we really bridged, we really developed a whole new world on campus. And I think that totally shaped how, I'm a businesswoman now, those lessons you learn forever. Like Robert's Rules of Orders, like how to run a meeting. I'll be in meetings now and I'll say, "Uh no, like what kind of system are we following here." So, all of that stuff definitely comes into play and teaches you how to do those things and how those things are important.

Khashifa's experience outlines the multiple leadership roles she took on as an undergraduate member of her sorority. As a charter line member, she and her line sisters were crucial in establishing her chapter, including administrative tasks, financial stability, and the public perception of the organization. Khashifa also brings up the important role that BGLOs play, particularly on predominantly white campuses, in creating programming for the Black campus community. BGLO programming serves to combat the racially exclusive campus climates that often characterize these white campuses (Allen 2013). Through BGLO-led programming, Black and other non-white students feel a sense of belonging on their college campus. Therefore, the benefits of BGLO programming extend beyond BGLO members to positively affect all Black students (Patton et al. 2011). The leadership skills that Khashifa cultivated when establishing her chapter and implementing their innovative programming are skills she continues to use in her adult life.

Amber, a 31-year-old white sorority member, also discussed the leadership skills she learned within her sorority, and how that knowledge helped her to build up her resume and career experience, saying:

> I learned a lot about working with local businesses. I learned a lot about the business side, because we would have chapter meetings every other week, and so you conducted it with Robert's Rules of Order and do treasury reports, and things like that. So, it definitely gave me insight into the business side of an organization. It gave me some leadership experience.

Similarly, Keilana, a 28-year-old Laotian sorority member, also talked about the connection between the skills that she learned in leadership positions within the sorority and her eventual career path:

It's given me a lot of skills, like leadership. So, I was a part of a lot of organizations prior to [pledging], because of [a campus leadership retreat]. Prior to membership in the organization, I served in other leadership positions. But, in this particular role, it was just more serious and business oriented. So, it's taught me a lot about time management, business skills. Like we don't play, we need to do this right. And that's really translated to the work that I do. I work at a university so I try to communicate with my students who are planning organizations, like "Why are you doing this?" Just the leadership skills that I have learned from being a member of my sorority.

It is telling that many of the reflections about leadership opportunities provided through BGLOs come from the women that we spoke with. While men undoubtedly had many of the same responsibilities for leadership and over half of our respondents served leadership positions in their respective chapters, women more frequently identified leadership skills as one of the effects of their membership. Research finds that BGLOs provide Black women with opportunities for leadership training and positions that they otherwise do not have in other organizations (Greyerbiehl and Mitchell 2014; Harris 1998; Phillips 2005). BGLOs also provide a space for women to cultivate community and their leadership abilities outside the competition of men (Mitchell 2014). We find that the opportunity for gendered leadership extended outside the Black community to non-Black members as well.

A Lifetime Commitment: Career Choices and Community Engagement

One main distinguishing feature of BGLOs as opposed to other types of fraternal organizations is the expectation of lifelong commitment to the organization. BGLOs, in turn, recognize members even in death. After a member dies, chapter members hold a special ceremony to induct that member into the organization's Omega Chapter. Through this ceremonial initiation, BGLOs pay homage to the work the member dedicated themselves to throughout their life. Moreover, the ceremony also demonstrates that the bonds of sisterhood and brotherhood remain unbroken even in death.

Because of the emphasis on commitment across the lifespan, members who join as undergraduates are expected to join a graduate chapter. In fact, virtually all of our respondents remained active in their BGLOs either at the local level or nationally, evidence of their ongoing commitment to community uplift. Quyen, the Vietnamese fraternity member, explains how BGLO membership instilled a passion for lifelong community service:

I mean I think the process definitely changed me and then I noticed how much work it took to actually be a [member of my fraternity]. And so I got more, I want to say I definitely got more heavily involved in community service work through [my fraternity]. I mean that kind of jump-started a lot of it … At the time it was really more focused on I'm gonna become a [member of the organization], I'm gonna show this dude [who belittled his ambition to become a member]. That was the initial purpose. And then after becoming [a member], it slowly changed to actually doing good deeds, good work for people. Helping out others. I mean, I did [community service] in high school but it was more so you gotta, kind of pad your resume to get into college. But after that, I feel like when I was applying for work they didn't really care about that kind of stuff. But I did it anyway just because, I would say [my fraternity] helped push me, helped push my focus on doing community service work.

Even though one of Quyen's initial motivations for membership was superficial and aimed at proving wrong those who doubted his commitment to his fraternity, through the meaningful relationships with other members, he found his intentions were transformed. The goals of the organization and the brotherhood of committed men became inscribed into his own perspective and it "helped push [his] focus on doing community service work." Although fraternities in general are often criticized for being purely social organizations, through Quyen's example we see that BGLOs have additional benefits that go beyond allegiance to a party culture on campus.

For Quyen and the other non-Black BGLO members we spoke with, membership instilled a desire for ongoing community engagement through service work. Roano, a 38-year-old Puerto Rican fraternity member, worked to push his fraternity to broaden its ideas of which communities are helped in their service and the types of service that they provide:

Some of our brothers sometimes come across as if the Civil Rights Movement and all of the work that our forefathers have done has only been for the Black community. I also remind our brothers that had it not been for those conversations we would not have made progress in the Women's Rights Movement, if you will. And for me, personally, today, [an] argument I think that exists, we still have not finished our conversation and work as it relates to equity and equality for African Americans. But the primary human rights issue in my mind today is about immigration and the Latino movement that is happening in the U.S. So I take personal interest and personal responsibility in making sure that my fraternity understands our obligation and responsibility as it relates to human rights in this country and what we need to be doing in partnership with other organizations or as an organization. We have fraternity brothers who are of Mexican American descent, who are of Central and South American descent, who are dealing with deportation and dealing with issues of citizenship, and I think our fraternity needs to take a look at how do we manage that conversation.

Roano makes the connection between injustices against the Black community and women, and immigration and Latinos. For Roano, he understands his BGLO as committed to a broader mission of human rights, not only Black equality. His specific focus on Latinos may reflect the linked fights for justice between Black and Brown communities. There may be an expectation of the linked fate between the communities, wherein people of color from different racial or ethnic groups are urged to advocate and fight for each other's particular issues. While he draws upon Latino fraternity members as one reason why his BGLO should be engaged in immigration rights advocacy, he goes on to make parallels to immigration issues facing other Black populations.

> The other piece that I often tell brothers is that the issue of immigration and human rights today is not just about Latinos. We have a large number of Haitian brothers who deal with immigration. We have brothers from different countries in the Caribbean who deal with immigration issues on a regular basis. So my argument or my thought or my reminder, if you will, to our brothers is we do not limit our conversation as it relates to human rights, civil rights, being a political voice and a financial voice for the different movements that are happening today. Our history book is beautiful but it is incomplete. And I think that sometimes it's important to remind our brothers that we can't just have a seat because we have arrived. There's still work to be done.

Roano drives home his argument for his fraternity's involvement with immigration rights by demonstrating the direct link between the issue and fraternity brothers who are members of the African diaspora. In doing so, this may be an attempt to frame his argument through a U.S.-based perception of Blackness, but also his argument alludes to a larger debate around the relevance of BGLOs. Although some inside and outside Black Greek organizations may believe that racial equality has been achieved in the contemporary era and that BGLOs are therefore no longer relevant or needed, Roano underlines that "there's still work to be done," and thus, that BGLOs are still necessary.

For some, this commitment to community service also translated into which career trajectories they chose. Charisse, the Filipina sorority member, explains:

> I think that it's impacted me in wanting to really give back to the community. And 'cause right now as an architecture student, I'm about to graduate and one of the biggest things that I was able to learn, like, you know, throughout our community service is just the fact of giving back. I'm privileged in attending college and gaining all of this knowledge and not many people get to do that. And so, for me I feel like I see myself wanting to give back even more and really transcribing that throughout my career. And so, my career plan so far is wanting to take architectural design and really implementing that with community design and helping create a social and economic

environment change throughout many communities ... "Service to all mankind" has really transcribed to my career goal.

"To be supreme in service to all mankind" is one of Alpha Kappa Alpha Sorority, Incorporated's creeds. As Charisse explains in this passage, she has incorporated this ideal into her future career. She cites the importance of using the knowledge that she has through her collegiate education to directly impact communities in need. Further, she merges her architecture education with community service through community design and development. In this way, her commitment to her sorority's mission is not solely an extracurricular activity, but rather integrated throughout her approach to life. Audra, a 21-year-old white sorority member, also describes how her BGLO membership has illuminated a connection between her educational interests and community involvement.

> I've been able to serve the community; it's much more meaningful now. I think it's also just given me a sense of responsibility and it has kind of changed my priorities in terms of, I guess, I'll say this, I'm a political science major, and so I definitely think people could blame me for exploiting [my sorority], but it's really just, as I look at all of the inequalities of our society and just ways that our country really needs to be improved. I always knew that lifting up the African American community would be important, but now I think it's more important than ever.

Although Audra previously identified the importance of programs targeting the African American community, her BGLO membership reaffirmed the priority of such programs and policies. Audra alludes to her membership providing more nuance to what she has learned as a political science major, but also highlights the precarious position she holds as a white BGLO member. Her motivations for membership are often questioned, with some assuming that she is in her sorority for personal gain only or "exploiting" her organization. Audra's comments also underscore common concerns and motivations among some of the white women BGLO members that we spoke with who have an initial hesitancy to be involved in racial justice efforts because of their positionality as white women. For these women, their membership in a Black organization provides a tangible connection to the Black community that moves their community service efforts from an optional activity to a moral imperative. In this way, BGLO membership allows them the ability to participate in actions and events that they might otherwise have felt uncomfortable with.

While Charisse and Audra described how their BGLO membership and community service have shaped their eventual career goals, other respondents described how their current careers are a direct result of their BGLO membership. Isabella, a 40-year-old Dominican sorority member, succinctly illustrates this point, stating, "I became a university administrator because of my involvement in Greek life." Thomas, the Vietnamese-Filipino fraternity member, went into more detail, explaining:

> [Membership] definitely shifted my identity to be a lot more racially conscious and aware and it brought me to where I am today, working in student affairs or aspiring to work in higher education administration. The founder of our chapter is one of the deans of students at [my university]. He became a really close mentor of mine. I still stay in touch with him. Actually, I'm gonna call him later this afternoon just to catch up. He's a professional and fraternal mentor to me. He also pushed me to work in this area but also provided me with like the connections to other brothers who may help me with interview practice and recommendations and advice and all that stuff. That solidified my identity as an aspiring educator and someone who looks to improve our future through the education of young folks.

Similarly, Hao, a 35-year-old Vietnamese fraternity member, shared: "[BGLO membership] also helped me establish a lot of connections, and so my first job at a college was actually through a connection of one of my fraternity brothers, and so that networking experience is, you know, ridiculously wide."

Once BGLO members, respondents joined an international network of brothers or sisters that could potentially facilitate their career advancement. Racial uplift does not only entail service to the Black community at large but also direct networking among members. Thomas's example of professional mentoring and connections provided through one of his chapter founders illustrates the net-working potential available through BGLO membership. Black fraternities and sororities provide a wealth of social capital (for example, actual and potential resources provided through social networks) for their members (Harper 2008; McClure 2006; Schuh et al. 1992; for more on social capital, see Bourdieu 1977, 1986, 1987).

Similar to our respondents' reflections, previous research finds that BGLO alumni are instrumental in providing both general guidance in the job market as well as targeted assistance, such as securing interviews or making introductions hiring managers. In examining the network-building benefits of BGLO fraternities to members, research finds that fraternity and sorority membership is especially fruitful for job searches post-undergraduate (Berkowitz and Padavic 1999). Members often enter their particular organization with job networking and pro-fessional development in mind, aiming to network with and be mentored by successful and professional Black alumni.

Family Matters: Bridging Racial Divides in the Family

The non-Black members of BGLOs that we spoke with shared how their mem-bership affected their personal growth, whether through increased self-esteem and confidence, leadership training, or career choices and community service commitment. However, some of these members, especially those who were second-generation Asian American, also revealed how their membership challenged those around them to grow. In particular, BGLO membership defied cultural expectations and challenged family members' racial perceptions about Blacks.

As we discussed previously, the majority of our respondents had little exposure to Black Greek life prior to college. Because of this, their family members were also typically unfamiliar with Greek life in general, and Black Greek life in particular. This lack of familiarity led to difficulties explaining their motivation or intentions to pledge these Black organizations for these respondents. For example, Quyen, the Vietnamese fraternity member, explained how he told his parents about his BGLO membership:

> [W]hen I told them, I knew they'd be awkward. They wouldn't really understand. So I told them, "Hey, I'm joining a multicultural fraternity." They're like, "Oh, ok. What does that mean?" I was just like, "Oh that's just what it is. It's everybody." So then they actually, they come to my campus, and I lived in the fraternity house. And they come and see it. I'm like, "Oh yeah, I live here. This is a Black fraternity." I just told them because my parents, they're, like I said, you know the stereotypes about Asians. They want you to make the grades and study hard. So, you being in a fraternity, in the first part, is not probably something they want to hear … Asian culture is about Asian people and they want you to stay within the Asian community.

Several of our second-generation Asian American respondents echoed this sentiment, noting that joining a Greek-letter organization was culturally unexpected or even disappointing. Their parents' expectations were often that they would focus solely on their educational pursuits while in college and not extracurricular activities which could be distracting. As Quyen's statement alludes to, the fact that the fraternity he joined was historically Black compounded his parents' disapproval of his choice. The awkwardness that Quyen anticipated from his parents was likely a mixture of his defying cultural and familial expectations in terms of going Greek, as well as crossing the color-line in an unexpected way. Given researchers' and the general public's assumption that equates success with assimilating into whiteness, especially for Asian Americans who are often termed a 'model minority,' our second-generation respondents' association with Blackness is likely an affront to their parents' assumed goals. Thomas, the Vietnamese-Filipino fraternity member, also made this connection between his parents' reaction to his BGLO membership and their desire for him to assimilate into (white) American culture. He expounded:

> [T]hey don't want to rock the boat. They want to avoid talking about race as it competes with predominantly majority white culture, and they really

value Asian American-ness but it's more about doing as what others do. So, in a way, they really, they are still, I would say that they were very confused at my decision to be an Alpha at the start. But, I think they've just gotten used to it over time.

Thomas's experience captures the difference between first-generation and second-generation Asian Americans' understanding of race and assimilation. For members of the first generation, being 'American' is associated with being white. This often includes adopting anti-Black attitudes as a strategy to assert their American-ness. For members of the second generation, experiences and aware-ness of their racialization as 'foreigners' may make them reject the expectation of assimilation into whiteness (Tuan 1998).

For some of our respondents, their parents' confusion and initial disapproval at their BGLO membership stemmed from negative depictions of Black Americans that their parents learned through media. Keung, a 30-year-old Chinese-Cambodian fraternity member, summed it up succinctly stating: "What they see on TV is what they believe. So, there's almost determinate discrimination and stereotypical views from that side because all they see is what's on TV." In fact, research finds a connection between media exposure and negative racial attitudes towards Blacks. For example, exposure to network news has been linked to increased endorsement of stereotypes and prejudicial attitudes about Blacks (Dixon 2008).

Non-Black BGLO members struggled with how to challenge and confront their families' beliefs and attitudes about Blackness. Keung went on to explain how he tries to combat the media images and his parents' insular social network by introducing his parents to his fraternity brothers: "I try to bring home my friends [from my fraternity] every now and then too so they can see that what you see on TV is not what's out there." Although Keung attempts to counter the negative media portrayals of Blacks by introducing his parents to individual fraternity brothers, it is unlikely that these introductions have changed his parents' attitudes about Blacks in general. Individual, sporadic cross-racial con-tact does not lead to transformation of prejudicial attitudes about a racial group (Jackman and Crane 1986). Instead, a multiplicity of meaningful and intimate relationships is necessary to produce change in attitudes (Davies et al. 2011; Ellison et al. 2011).

Beyond passive educational attempts, some of our respondents shared explicit actions they took to challenge their parents' racial views. Quyen, the Vietna-mese fraternity member, described pushing back against his parents' critiques about his decision to fraternize with Black Americans, stating, "I would basically push back right in front of them." While Quyen's parents seemed to be more open to these differences in opinions, for other respondents, this was not the case. Keilana, the Laotian sorority member, explained how her disagreement with her family's racist views and this desire to educate them led to separation between herself and family members:

> [M]y family didn't teach me about some of the racism and prejudice that would go on in the world, I had to teach them … [I]t was important to me for my family not [to] be racist, prejudice[d], and so it was so bad that my favorite uncle and I didn't talk for a while … It was to the point where I did not speak with him for years.

As Keilana's quote illustrates, there are social costs for defying family-held beliefs. Though defying elders is generally discouraged across cultures, within Asian cultures this expectation of adhering to elders is heightened. Compounding Keilana's disregard for tradition is her position as a woman. She therefore viewed as disrespecting both age and gender expectations. In her commitment to anti-racism, Keilana is not only taking a principled stand for something but also against tradition. Eventually, she and her uncle reconciled and he became an instrumental source of family support, even facilitating other family members' acceptance of her Black fiancé.

The decision to cross racial lines and join a BGLO cannot be evaluated lightly. For the second-generation Asian American respondents in this section, their membership in a fraternity or sorority was already a transgression of cultural expectations; adding in the race-based nature of the organizations intensified the confusion. Family members' displeasure at their BGLO membership was rooted in a combination of cultural expectations regarding the purpose of a college education and ideals around who one should fraternize with. Moreover, these ideals were influenced by racial cues from media and other secondary sources.

BGLOs' eternal bonds of brotherhood and sisterhood and dedication to community uplift are collectivist orientations. Therefore, although BGLO membership may seem at odds with assimilation expectations, it may actually be harmonious with Asian culture's collectivist ideology. In fact, research finds that second-generation Vietnamese Americans use the ideology of collectivism to "form and recapture their ethnic identity" (Thai 2002:76). Through BGLO membership, second-generation Asian American members may be merging cultural values with racialization that marks them as racially othered. In this way, second-generation Asian American BGLO membership is in line with theories of the new second generation that predict multiple types of assimilation. For example, instead of only aiming for assimilation into whiteness, theories of segmented assimilation posit that members of the second generation may also assimilate into the underclass or preserve their immigrant community's values (Portes and Zhou 1993). Among the second-generation BGLO members that we spoke with, we see an identification with Black Americans, who are positioned at the bottom of U.S. racial stratification, but also a continued expression of their ethnic identity through connections to collectivism.

Conclusion

Amid debates about the relevancy and benefits of membership in Black fraternities and sororities, we find that BGLO membership results in multiple positive outcomes for our respondents. The initial goal of lifelong bonds of brotherhood or sisterhood was fulfilled. Additionally, we found three categories of personal-level benefits: self-confidence and a stronger voice in speaking out against injustice, a connection to a long heritage of leadership and service with the personal responsibility to continue that legacy, and a commitment to community uplift not only through BGLO membership but career choices as well.

Respondents' increased self-confidence in their own capabilities and their ability to speak out was directly tied to their membership process and the bond with their fellow BGLO members. The affinity they felt for their BGLO extended to key historic members. Through this connection to prominent BGLO members who were instrumental to securing civil rights, our respondents harbored a responsibility to continue to work towards equality. Their commitment to do so led to the cultivation of leadership skills that often prepared them for life post-college. In addition to continued commitment to community uplift through their BGLOs' nationally designated initiatives, some respondents integrated service into their career goals. Some were able to make connections between their educational pursuits, such as architecture or political science, and community justice. Others were inspired by their BGLO membership to pursue careers in higher education. In addition to BGLO membership influencing community engagement and career commitments, BGLO members affected their respective organizations through attempts to broaden their organization's commitment to social justice.

One unintended family-level outcome was the effect of BGLO membership on family members' understanding of race and racism among our second-generation Asian American respondents. The racial bridging conducted by these respondents calls attention to the persistence of racialized scripts negatively portraying Black Americans. Residential areas, much like college campuses, continue to be racially segregated, decreasing the likelihood of meaningful and sustained interpersonal interactions that would combat these negative portrayals. While BGLO membership may be a culturally and racially unexpected decision for our Asian American respondents, as well as other respondents, on the racially divisive college campuses, this choice is a rational response to the racial divide.

Our Asian American respondents' family relations highlight the tensions that often exist when occupying multiple group memberships. In Chapter 2, we discussed how respondents navigate their non-Black identity as members of Black networks. However, here we see how Asian American respondents navigate their identity as BGLO members among their Asian family members. Although some may have concealed their membership initially, these respondents did not discard their BGLO membership, relegating it to BGLO spaces only, but instead eventually integrated this aspect of their identity into the family realm. Though the social costs were high, in some cases leading to distance within the family, addressing family members' racist views was worth the risk.

Among our other respondents, however, very few of our white respondents mentioned addressing friends' or family members' prejudicial or racist views.

White respondents often mentioned experiencing teasing from white friends about their affiliation with Black people or general awareness of the prejudicial views about Black people held by family members. White respondents may have felt that countering their friends' and family members' views would lead to further ostracism than what they already experienced due to their BGLO membership. Still other white respondents explicitly stated that they did not have the 'time or energy' to engage in race-related conversations with their family members, instead stating that overcoming prejudice is the individual believer's own responsibility. This view may be a reflection of Western individualism. Individualistic orientation emphasizes individual initiative and achievement and de-emphasizes community uplift. Overall, white respondents demonstrate the challenges of resolving the discrepancies between their competing group memberships. Unlike our Asian American respondents, white respondents were unable to integrate their understanding of race and racism into their other realms of group membership, such as family.

In total, these personal-level and family-level impacts were often a result of the membership process coupled with the lifelong bonds created among respondents' line and fellow fraternity or sorority members. Particularly key were processes that facilitated in-group membership. Through the maintenance of symbolic boundaries, respondents not only felt a sense of belonging as BGLO members but also understood the particular values and beliefs of their respective organization and BGLO culture as a whole. Accordingly, although these beneficial outcomes are important to note for their transformational effects on the respondents and their family relations, they also demonstrate the persistence of racial discourse in the creation and maintenance of symbolic and social boundaries.

Notes

1 Delta Sigma Theta's first sorority action was to participate in a suffrage march on the eve of President Woodrow Wilson's inauguration in 1913. For a detailed account of Delta Sigma Theta's participation in the Women's Suffrage March, see Giddings 1988.
2 Mary McLeod Bethune was born on July 10, 1875, in Mayesville, South Carolina, a child of former slaves. In 1904, Bethune established the Daytona Normal and Industrial Institute for Negro Girls in Daytona, Florida. The Institute later merged with the Cookman Institute for Men and was renamed Bethune-Cookman College. She served as the president of the Florida chapter of the National Association of Colored Women, and in 1924, Bethune became the organization's national leader. Bethune also served as an advisor to several presidents: President Calvin Coolidge (child welfare); President Herbert Hoover (Commission on Home Building and Home Ownership; Committee on Child Health); and President Franklin D. Roosevelt (minority affairs; Director of the Division of Negro Affairs of the National Youth Administration). She established the National Council of Negro Women. Bethune passed away on May 18, 1955, in Daytona, Florida. For a more detailed biography, see Robertson and Boyd 2015.
3 Shirley Anita St. Hill Chisholm was born November 30, 1924, in Brooklyn, New York. She earned her Bachelor's degree from Brooklyn College in 1946 and her Master's degree in elementary education from Columbia University in 1952. In 1968, she

became the first African American congresswoman. She went on to serve seven terms in the House of Representatives representing New York's 12th Congressional District. She was one of the founding members of the Congressional Black Caucus. In 1972, Chisholm became the first major-party African American candidate to make a bid for the U.S. presidency, running for the Democratic nomination. She passed away on January 1, 2005, in Ormond Beach, Florida. For a more detailed biography, see Chisholm 2010.

4 Barbara Charline Jordan was born February 21, 1936, in Houston, Texas. She earned her Bachelor's degree from Texas Southern University in 1956 and her law degree from Boston University Law School in 1959. In 1966 she won a seat in the Texas Senate; she was the first African American state senator since 1883 and the first Black woman state senator. She was the first African American woman to serve as president pro tem of the state senate. In 1962, Jordan was elected to the U.S. House of Representatives. In 1994, President Bill Clinton appointed her to head the Commission on Immigration Reform. Jordan passed away on January 17, 1996, in Austin, Texas. For a more detailed biography, see Jordan 1979.

References

Allen, Shaonta' E. 2013. "Stomping The Yard In Black And White: A Comparative Study Of The Perceived Benefits Of Black Greek Life At Historically Black And Predominantly White Institutions," Master's Thesis, Department of Sociology, Middle Tennessee State University.

American Council on Human Rights, Commission on Evaluation. 1954. *The American Council on Human Rights: An Evaluation*. Washington, DC: The Council.

Berkowitz, Alexandra and Irene Padavic. 1999. "Getting a Man or Getting Ahead: A Comparison of White and Black Sororities." *Journal of Contemporary Ethnography* 27(4):530–557.

Borgonovi, Francesca. 2008. "Doing Well by Doing Good: The Relationship between Formal Volunteering and Self-Reported Health and Happiness." *Social Science & Medicine* 66(11):2321–2334.

Bourdieu, Pierre. 1977. "Cultural Reproduction and Social Reproduction." Pp. 487–511 in *Power and Ideology in Education*, edited by J. Karabel and A.H. Halsey. New York, NY: Oxford University Press.

Bourdieu, Pierre. 1986. "The Forms of Capital." Pp. 241–258 in *Handbook of Theory and Research for the Sociology of Education*, edited by J.G. Richardson. Westport, CT: Greenwood.

Bourdieu, Pierre. 1987. "What Makes a Social Class? On the Theoretical and Practical Existence of Groups." *Berkeley Journal of Sociology* 32(1):1–17.

Chisholm, Shirley. 2010. *Unbought and Unbossed: Expanded 40th Anniversary Edition*. Take Root Media.

Davies, Kristin, Linda R. Tropp, Arthur Aron, Thomas F. Pettigrew, and Stephen C. Wright. 2011. "Cross-Group Friendships and Intergroup Attitudes: A Meta-Analytic Review." *Personality and Social Psychology Review* 15(4):332–351.

Dixon, Travis L. 2008. "Network News and Racial Beliefs: Exploring the Connection between National Television News Exposure and Stereotypical Perceptions of African Americans." *Journal of Communication* 58(2):321–337.

Ellison, Christopher G., Heeju Shin, and David L. Leal. 2011. "The Contact Hypothesis and Attitudes Towards Latinos in the United States." *Social Science Quarterly* 92(4):938–958.

Erwin, Erin, Camille Jones, Tom Kilian, and Lisa Woodie. 2004. "Understanding Satisfaction: The Effect of Black Greek-Letter Organization Membership on African American College Students at a Predominantly White Institution." *Journal of the Indiana Student Personnel Association*:67–81.

Fine, Elizabeth C. 2003. *Soulstepping: African American Step Shows*. Urbana, IL: University of Illinois Press.

Giddings, Paula. 1988. *In Search of Sisterhood: Delta Sigma Theta and the Challenge of the Black Sorority Movement*. New York, NY: Morrow.

Graham, David A. 2015. "The Mysterious Death of Freddie Gray." *The Atlantic*, April 22. Retrieved from www.theatlantic.com/politics/archive/2015/04/the-mysterious-death-of-freddie-gray/391119/.

Greyerbiehl, Lindsay and Donald Mitchell Jr. 2014. "An Intersectional Social Capital Analysis of the Influence of Historically Black Sororities on African American Women's College Experiences at a Predominantly White Institution." *Journal of Diversity in Higher Education* 7(4):282–294.

Harper, Shaun R. 2008. "Realizing the Intended Outcomes of Brown: High-achieving African American Male Undergraduates and Social Capital." *American Behavioral Scientist* 51(7):1030–1053.

Harris, Felecia C. 1998. "Community Service in Academia: The Role of African American Sisterhood in the 1990s." *Journal of General Education* 47(4):282–301.

Hernandez, Marcia and Gregory S. Parks. 2016. "Fortitude in the Face of Adversity: Delta Sigma Theta's History of Racial Uplift. " *Hastings Race & Poverty Law Journal* 13:273.

Jackman, Mary R. and Marie Crane. 1986. "'Some of my best friends are black…': Interracial Friendship and Whites' Racial Attitudes." *Public Opinion Quarterly* 50(4):459–486.

Jordan, Barbara. 1979. *Barbara Jordan: A Self-Portrait*. New York, NY: Doubleday.

Kimbrough, Walter M. 1995. "Self-assessment, Participation, and Value of Leadership Skill, Activities, and Experiences for Black Students Relative to Their Membership in Historically Black Fraternities and Sororities." *Journal of Negro Education* 64(1):63–74.

Kimbrough, Walter M. 2003. *Black Greek 101: The Culture, Customs, and Challenges of Black Fraternities and Sororities*. Lanham, MD: Farleigh Dickinson University Press.

Kimbrough, Walter M. and Philo A. Hutcheson 1998. "The Impact of Student Membership in Black Greek-Letter Organizations on Black Students' Involvement in Collegiate Activities and Their Development of Leadership Skills." *Journal of Negro Education* 67(2):96–105.

Laybourn, Wendy Marie and Gregory S. Parks. 2016a. "Brotherhood and the Quest for African American Social Equality: A Story of Phi Beta Sigma." *Maryland Law Journal, Race, Religion, Gender & Class* 16(1):1–47.

Laybourn, Wendy Marie and Gregory S. Parks. 2016b. "The Sons of Indiana: Kappa Alpha Psi and the Fight for Civil Rights." *Indiana Law Journal* 91(4):1425–1472.

Laybourn, Wendy Marie and Gregory S. Parks. 2016c. "Omega Psi Phi Fraternity and the Fight for Civil Rights." *Wake Forest Journal of Law and Policy* 6(1):213–301.

McClure, Stephanie M. 2006. "Voluntary Association Membership: Black Greek Men on a Predominantly White Campus." *The Journal of Higher Education* 77(6):1037–1057.

Mitchell, Jr., Donald. 2014. "Does Gender Matter in Black Greek-Letter Organizations?" *Oracle* 9(1):20–32.

Parks, Gregory S. and Caryn Neumann. 2015. "Lifting as They Climb: Race, Sorority, and African American Uplift in the 20th Century." *Hastings Women's Law Journal* 27:109–144.

Parks, Gregory S., Rashawn Ray, and Shawna M. Patterson. 2014. "Complex Civil Rights Organizations: Alpha Kappa Alpha Sorority, An Exemplar." *Wake Forest Univ. Legal Studies* Paper No. 2537160.

Patton, Lori D., Brian K. Bridges, and Lamont A. Flowers. 2011. "Effects of Greek Affiliation on African American Students' Engagement: Differences by College Racial Composition." *College Student Affairs Journal* 29(2):113–123.

Phillips, Clarenda M. 2005. "Sisterly Bonds: African American Sororities Rising to Overcome Obstacles." Pp. 341–359 in *African American Fraternities and Sororities: The Legacy and the Vision*, edited by T.L. Brown, G.S. Parks, and C.M. Phillips. Lexington, KY: University Press of Kentucky.

Portes, Alejandro and Min Zhou. 1993. "The New Second Generation: Segmented Assimilation and Its Variants Among Post-1965 Immigrant Youth." *The ANNALS of the American Academy of Political and Social Science* 530(1):74–98.

Ray, Rashawn. 2013. "Fraternity Life at Predominantly White Universities in the US: The Saliency of Race." *Ethnic and Racial Studies* 36(2):320–336.

Reason, Robert D., Elizabeth A. Roosa Miller, and Tara C. Scales. 2005. "Toward a Model of Racial Justice Ally Development." *Journal of College Student Development* 46(5):530–546.

Robertson, Ashley N. and Gwendolyn Boyd. 2015. *Mary McLeod Bethune in Florida: Bringing Social Justice to the Sunshine State.* Mount Pleasant, SC: Arcadia Publishing.

Schuh, John H., Vicky L. Triponey, Lynette L. Heim, and Karyn Nishimura. 1992. "Student Involvement in Historically Black Greek Letter Organizations." *NASPA Journal* 29:274–282.

Sutton, E. Michael and Walter M. Kimbrough. 2001. "Trends in Black Student Involvement." *NASPA Journal* 39(1):30–34.

Sutton, E. Michael and Melvin C. Terrell. 1997. "Identifying and Developing Leadership Opportunities for African American Men." Pp. 55–64 in *Helping African American Men Succeed in College. New Directions for Student Services*, edited by M.J. Cuyjet. San Francisco, CA: Jossey Bass.

Thai, Hung Cam. 2002. "Formation of Ethnic Identity among Second Generation Vietnamese Americans" Pp. 53–84 in *Second Generation Ethnic Identity among Asian Americans*, edited by P.G. Min. Walnut Creek, CA: AltaMira Press.

Thoits, Peggy A. and Lyndi N. Hewitt. 2001. "Volunteer Work and Well-Being." *Journal of Health and Social Behavior* 42(2):115–131.

Tuan, Mia. 1998. *Forever Foreigners or Honorary Whites: The Asian Ethnic Experience Today.* New Brunswick, NJ: Rutgers University Press.

Wilson, John. 2000. "Volunteering." *Annual Review of Sociology* 26:215–240.

CONCLUSION

"I'm Not the First, and I Won't Be the Last": Crossing the Line, Connecting the Past and Present

[In the ideal collegiate situation] there is a Zeta in a girl regardless of race, creed, or color, who has high standards and principles, a good scholarly average and an active interest in all things that she undertakes to accomplish.

Viola Tyler, Founder, Zeta Phi Beta

[O]ne of my founders did make a very public statement, and I know every non-Black member in Zeta runs to that statement that our founder said of, "Regardless of race, creed, or color, there's a Zeta girl in every woman." But you know what, in all honesty, if she was willing to make that statement in the [19]20s, [19]30s then why [today] are we still having such a problem with it?

Stacey, 30-year-old white sorority member

Why *does* racial integration continue to be controversial? Our exploration into non-Black members of Black fraternities and sororities sheds light on a particular facet of this question. As Stacey asks, even though Black Greek-letter organizations (BGLOs) have a longstanding tradition of integrationist values, why are people "still having such a problem" with the concept of non-Black membership? In examining a highly visible, often contentious, and generally unexpected form of crossing the color-line, we found the persistence of divisive racial thinking. In particular, one enduring racial expectation is that racial group members will socialize among their own group. If and when they do not, there are certain rules that guide acceptable forms of cross-racial association. Most commonly when racial integration is discussed, the conversation is centered around Blacks, or other marginalized racial groups, assimilating into whiteness. This viewpoint exemplifies a white racial frame, a meaning system held by many white Americans that conditions and reinforces the superiority of whiteness (Feagin 2009).

In contrast, the concept of whites integrating into Blackness remains unorthodox, incomprehensible, and confusing to many. Moreover, when discussion is about other marginalized racial groups, such as Asians or Latinos, integrating into Blackness, it is conceived of as downward assimilation, or as evidence of the failure of the ability of these racial groups to integrate successfully in society. The subject matter within this book is unique within those that focus on racial integration. In contrast to studies that build upon the normalizing assumption of non-whites crossing into whiteness, we investigate the process of non-Blacks crossing the color-line into Blackness. The integration patterned by the non-Black BGLO members that we spoke to challenges the one-directional viewpoint of racial integration.

What Non-Black BGLO Members Tell Us About Race

Racial integration is often characterized as signaling the dissolution of barriers to racial justice. That is, if more people could cross the racial lines that they face in everyday life, by moving into an integrated neighborhood, marrying interracially, or making friends of different races, the assumption is that the state of race relations in the United States would improve greatly. This ideal is built on the premise that increasing cross-racial contact will enhance racial understandings, empathy, and connection across racial lines, as exemplified by contact theory (Pettigrew 1998). Taking this viewpoint, the 34 non-Black BGLO members we talked to might seem like model racial citizens, driven to join an intimate cross-racial organization and authentically envelop themselves in a racial group and history not their own. According to contact theory, these positive interactions should be a major step toward improved racial relations.

However, as we document through this book, crossing racial boundaries is not such a simple process. Instead, we find that symbolic boundaries do not easily reconfigure even through cross-racial contact. So what do non-Black members of BGLOs tell us about race in the contemporary U.S.? The members we spoke to help to demonstrate the rigidity of racial symbolic boundaries; the persistence of the white racial frame; the overlapping and contradictory multiple configurations of the racial stratification system; and the perils of weak diversity.

Racial Symbolic Boundaries

The experiences of non-Black BGLO members illuminate the processes and practices in racial boundary crossing, and how individuals navigate multiple and competing racial boundaries, as these members come to understand themselves as non-Blacks who are associated with and connected to Blackness. Due to the rigid boundaries around race and socialization, non-Black members of Black fraternities and sororities experienced opposition from Black members of their organizations, as well as co-ethnics outside them. While some Black BGLO members were accepting, others approached their membership with hesitancy or outright rejection, holding the view that BGLOs are "for Blacks only." Those around them viewed crossing racial lines as unexpected, confusing, and/or calling into question their racial allegiance. It is less likely that our non-white, non-Black respondents would have experienced the same backlash had they joined historically white organizations, highlighting the expectations for assimilation into whiteness by people of color and the perpetuation of white superiority.

However, despite the pushback that they received, non-Black BGLO members reported that their organizational membership strengthened or expanded their conceptions of their racial identity. Contrary to popular belief that non-Black members of BGLOs are "trying to be Black," respondents expressed a strong racial identity, albeit a more nuanced one. Unlike research on non-white members of white Greek-letter organizations which finds non-white members are stereotyped and tokenized by their fellow sorority and fraternity members, this was typically not the case among our non-Black BGLO members. We also illuminated other long-term effects of BGLO membership, such as increased self-esteem, confidence, and connections to social justice whether through community engagement or career choices. Taken together they highlight broader ideas about race, identity, and group boundaries, particularly as they pertain to race relations and racial hierarchy in the contemporary U.S.

In sum, crossing a color-line is not enough to transform the meaning of race. Instead, we see that color-line crossers are enveloped within racialized logics that explain away their boundary crossing and their racial group membership; in this case, non-Blacks became 'Blackened' by their BGLO membership, and their position as 'true' or 'authentic' members of their own racial group is challenged. The effects of integration appear to be localized, calling into question the viability of individual integration.

White Racial Frame

Through their BGLO membership, some non-Black members were awakened to a system of racism and discrimination around them, which differed from the normalization of marginalization of non-white people that they had been exposed to prior to pledging their organization. For some respondents, particularly the Asian and Latino respondents, this understanding of white supremacy led them to see their fate tied to other marginalized racial groups. In this way, their BGLO membership was an expression of this belief in commonality across racial lines.

Through the pervasiveness of the white racial frame, we also see that Blackness continues to serve as a reference group for other racial groups. It is against Blackness that others are able to craft their racial identity and racialized place within society. For whites, doing so positions them as a normative in-group and Blacks as an out-group. This framing is what accounts for whites' rejection of white BGLO members. In regards to other racialized groups, Blackness serves as a reference in similar and different ways. Similar to the construction of the out-group for whites, Blacks serve the same role, particularly for those groups and individuals wishing to assimilate into whiteness. In a different manner, however, Blackness serves as a reference group for understanding oneself as a member of a marginalized group. In particular, many of our second-generation Asian American respondents expressed coming to a deeper understanding of their own racialization and place in U.S. society through their relationships with their Black brothers and sisters.

Despite the nuance that non-Black BGLO members bring to thinking about racial integration and the color-line, we find that these same members hold onto vestiges of the white racial frame. Even while they are identified as racial boundary transgressors, we find that some non-Black members engage in substantial rationalization to reimagine their BGLOs as colorblind spaces. These members drew upon a colorblind logic to explain their membership even as they often acknowledged the distinctly race-specific founding and mission of their organization. Ironically, some members expressed a colorblind approach *after* becoming members though they initially understood the organization as specifically race-based.

This finding brings together the literatures on colorblindness and color consciousness in racial boundary crossing. Whereas some research has documented that those who cross racial boundaries engage in colorblind ideology (Bonilla-Silva 2002), others find that these individuals actually work to highlight the racialized dimensions and structures within institutions (Hunter and Hughey 2013). However, we document instances of both within the non-Black members we spoke to, illuminating that neither approach seems to adequately disentangle how those actively seeking to cross racial lines are able still to hold colorblind views. Our contention is that to fully understand this paradox, researchers must examine each individual's multiple, and often competing, group memberships. Interrogating how individuals navigate these group memberships may highlight the tension that occurs within social group identities. Doing so has implications for understanding how those who cross racial boundaries are able to hold seemingly contradictory ideologies.

Multiple Racial Stratification Systems

Although there is one overarching racial formation, the enactment of the racial order, such as Black–white, white/non-white, and Black/non-Black configurations, is contextually specific. Racial fault lines develop in response to the specific racial demographics and racial histories of various geographical areas. Contextually dependent racial stratification is one reason why some of our respondents experienced a "culture shock" when they left their hometown to attend college. In moving from the racial geography of their hometown, they found they also left the configuration of racial groups and racialized expectations they had taken for granted. They now had to learn to navigate a different racial landscape.

Given the context-specific nature of racial stratification, people navigate their position based on the spaces they find themselves in and the concomitant racial norms. Even if the prevailing racial expectations are not the individual's own understanding of herself, she still must be knowledgeable about where she fits into the racial landscape in order to navigate it successfully. Understanding the racial order allows people to formulate their identities and their relationships in ways to potentially empower themselves against it.

Respondents' own meaning-making in regards to their membership sheds light on how different members of racialized groups interpret racial stratification and how they then use that knowledge to affirm or transform their own racial identities and racial group membership. It also puts into relief the shortcomings of racial stratification theories that characterize racial hierarchy as a static configuration. By only focusing on one type of hierarchy, the ways in which race and racial classification respond to shifting racial demographics is ignored.

Perils of Weak Diversity

Finally, colorblindness and weak diversity do not prepare students for racial realities of unequal resources and disparate treatment by race, which they experience on their college campuses. Contemporary higher education is advertised as a space for diversity and inclusion, but respondents continued to report severe racial divides on their college campuses and the marginalization of people of color.

Weak diversity is an offshoot of multiculturalism. Although multiculturalism is used to refer to a multitude of ideas, in its most popular form it refers to a celebration of cultural difference that simultaneously promotes assimilation. Weak diversity, the contemporary reincarnation of multiculturalism, extends this line of thinking to a celebration of any difference. With this focus, weak diversity masks differential power relations between racialized groups while diverting attention away from structural racial inequalities. Higher education's weak diversity is most clearly evidenced in university recruitment materials which overemphasize the degree to which different raced, gendered, or ability students are present, interact with one another, and the degree to which colleges and university center those experiences.

While weak diversity touts preparing students for the 'real world,' one that is increasingly multiracial, in fact, students are less prepared to handle the racial realities on their own campuses. Despite a lack of support by administration for meaningful attention to racial issues, for some students these issues are paramount. As a result, many students, like our respondents, turn to student-led organizations to make sense of and attempt to address the racial inequalities around them. Students continue to be engaged with organizations that attend to the racial climate on their campus, address the surrounding community's needs, and provide a space for addressing broader social justice issues. In this way, BGLOs may serve as one space of strong diversity wherein racial inequalities are acknowledged and addressed. As many of our respondents demonstrate, through BGLO membership their own racial identities were affirmed and strengthened rather than diminished or tokenized.

Crossing the Line: A Paradox

Our analysis of non-Black BGLO members gestures towards a paradoxical dynamic. Similar to a previous study (Hughey 2008), we find that non-Black members engage in distinct rhetorical and discursive strategies to make sense of their boundary crossing. In particular, our findings demonstrate members' awareness of boundary crossing both into their BGLOs and outside expectations of their own racial groups. By situating our findings within the literature on boundaries and racialized social systems, we are able to move beyond categorizing types of non-Black membership, and instead to interrogating the challenges and possibilities for full membership and concomitant symbolic boundary maintenance or redrawing.

Although initially appearing progressive and transformative by crossing the color-line into the marginalized arena of Blackness, all non-Black BGLO members must rationalize this choice by navigating, and in some cases reinforcing, the racial boundaries that they supposedly fight against. While some non-Black members utilize colorblind logic to eschew racial boundaries, some white members fully embraced racialized logics of white paternalism to emphasize that their whiteness gave them an imperative to cross the color-line and challenge social segregation. White respondents justified their logic by drawing upon a white racial frame that positions them in a paternal role while also denying their responsibility, or whites' responsibility, for racial animus. Moreover, although non-Black members of BGLOs often embody the problems associated with racial authenticity claims, the presence of non-Black members in BGLOs often reinforced and bolstered racial boundaries that associated BGLOs as only for Blackness to outsiders. Non-Black members were told that their membership was acceptable because they were "practically" or "almost" Black, even when the members did not identify that way. Therefore, instead of redefining the color-line and challenging racial boundaries within Greek life, non-Black members often reinforce rigid boundaries of Blackness.

This type of paradoxical boundary work in organizations is not unique to non-Blacks in BGLOs. Other research has documented that institutions that may initially appear transformative due to the crossing of racial boundaries perform considerable boundary work in order to maintain the racialized status quo. Childs (2002) reported that interracial couples utilize colorblind language to deny the importance of race in their family lives. Burke (2012) found that racially diverse communities utilize colorblind ideologies to recreate a white racial habitus. Hughey (2010) found that people of color who join white Greek-letter organizations do not assimilate racially, but rather perform stereotypical racialized identities in order to gain acceptance within their fraternal organizations. Interestingly, we find these same patterns emerge even amongst our non-Black members, who often bring considerable racial privilege to the sphere of Black Greek-letter organizations. This suggests that it is not so much the entrance into a group based on dominant identity that ends up restricting marginalized identities, but rather, that crossing any type of symbolic boundary often requires stereotypical or dominant ideologies for people to rationalize and make meaning of their actions.

★★★

Not too long ago Wendy was at a luncheon seated at a table with established race researchers and personnel from various diversity units. Though everyone was not personally acquainted prior to the lunch, the atmosphere was friendly and the conversation fast paced and upbeat. The conversation turned to non-Blacks in Black spaces and then the question of how they identify. Without skipping a beat, someone responded, "That's easy. They think they're Black!" Laughter erupted from around the table. Whether the retort was a personally held belief of the responder or simply a play on commonly held assumptions about non-Blacks who associate with Blacks, we may never know. Either way, the response and accompanying resounding laughter demonstrate the durability of these racialized beliefs even among those whose work centers around critical examinations of race.

It is often assumed that racial equality and justice hinge on those crossing racial boundaries and integrating informal and formal social circles. By contrast, our respondents' experiences, like the exchange at lunch, demonstrate that crossing the color-line into a Black fraternal organization is often accompanied by racist logics and stereotypes. Even as respondents' own racial identities were bolstered, blurred, or broadened, these changes did not transform larger racialized expectations. Moreover, our non-Black BGLO members' racial boundary work was largely contained within their local chapters, questioning the potential for widespread or institutional change spurring from individual-level challenges to racial boundaries. Even as non-Black members cross into BGLOs, the color-line itself is not easy to break.

References

Bonilla-Silva, Eduardo. 2002. "The Linguistics of Color Blind Racism: How to Talk Nasty about Blacks without Sounding 'Racist.'" *Critical Sociology* 28(1–2):41–64.

Burke, Meghan. 2012. "Discursive Fault Lines: Reproducing White Habitus in a Racially Diverse Community." *Critical Sociology* 38(5):645–668.

Childs, Erica Chito. 2002. "Families on the Color-Line: Patrolling Borders and Crossing Boundaries." *Race and Society* 5:139–161.

Feagin, Joe A. 2009. *The White Racial Frame*. New York, NY: Routledge.

Hughey, Matthew W. 2008. "'I did it for the brotherhood': Nonblack Members in Black Greek-letter Organizations." Pp. 313–343 in *Black Greek-letter Organizations in the Twenty-First Century: Our Fight Has Just Begun*, edited by G.S. Parks. Lexington, KY: University Press of Kentucky.

Hughey, Matthew W. 2010. "Paradox of Participation: Nonwhites in White Sororities and Fraternities." *Social Problems* 57(4):653–679.

Hunter, Joanna and Matthew W. Hughey. 2013. "'It's not written on their skin like it is ours': Greek-letter Organizations in the Age of the Multicultural Imperative." *Ethnicities* 13(5):519–543.

Pettigrew, Thomas F. 1998. "Intergroup Contact Theory." *Annu Rev Psychol* 49:65–85.

METHODOLOGICAL APPENDIX

TABLE A.1 Respondent Demographic Information

Pseudonym	Age	Racial identity	Gender	Home region	# of previous non-Blacks in Chapter	College type
Adam	39	White	Male	Northeast	0	N/A**
Alessandra	44	Guatemalan	Female	Northeast	4	Large public
Amber	31	White	Female	South	1	Large public
Antonio	24	Mexican	Male	West Coast	6	Medium public
Audra	21	White	Female	West Coast	0	Medium private
Bailey	24	White/Hispanic	Female	South	3	Large public
Binh	29	Vietnamese	Male	Southeast	0	Small private
Bradley	23	White	Male	Southeast	0	Large public
Carley	23	White/Egyptian	Female	Southwest	2	Large public
Charisse	23	Filipina	Female	South	1	Large public
Chris	22	White	Male	Southeast	3	Large public
Emma	23	White	Female	Southeast	0	Small private

Pseudonym	Age	Racial identity	Gender	Home region	# of previous non-Blacks in Chapter	College type
Hao	35	Vietnamese	Male	Southeast	3	Large public
Hazel	34	White	Female	South	0	Large public
Isabella	40	Dominican	Female	Northeast	4	Large private
Jasmine	32	Korean/Puerto Rican	Female	South	0	Large public
Jessica	22	White	Female	South	9	Medium private
John	30	Korean	Fluid	South	6	Large private
Justin	22	White	Male	West Coast	N/A★	Large private
Keilana	28	Laotian	Female	South	5	Large public
Kelly	42	White	Female	Midwest	0	N/A★★
Keung	30	Chinese/Cambodian	Male	Northeast	0	Large private
Khashifa	35	Pakistani	Female	Southeast	0	Large private
Michael	22	White	Male	South	5	Small private
Osita	33	Puerto Rican	Female	Southeast	0	N/A★★
Quyen	31	Vietnamese	Male	Southeast	1	Medium private
Roano	38	Puerto Rican	Male	Southeast	4	Medium public
Samantha	22	White	Female	Southeast	2	Medium private
Sofia	27	White/Hispanic	Female	South	0	Large public
Sri	37	Bangladeshi	Male	South	0	Large public
Stacey	30	White	Female	Southwest	1	Large public
Thomas	26	Vietnamese/Filipino	Male	West Coast	2	Medium private
Todd	20	Mexican/Japanese	Male	Southeast	1	Small private
Vicente	42	Puerto Rican	Male	Northeast	0	Medium public

N=34. ★ Charter line for BGLO chapter. ★★ Joined BGLO as graduate.

Interview Guide

I Reason for Membership

How did you decide to join a Greek-letter organization?

- Why a Black Greek-letter organization (BGLO)?
- Why not a multiracial or other race-based fraternal organization [e.g., Asian, Latino]?
- Did you always know you would join a Greek-letter organization?
- [if no] What made you decide to join a Greek organization, specifically a BGLO?
- How did you decide to join your BGLO and not another BGLO?

Were friends and/or family members in BGLOs?

- Members of other Greek-letter organizations?
- What were their reactions to your membership?

Do you remain active in your BGLO? Why or why not?

- [if no] Do you anticipate becoming active? Why or why not?
- [if yes] Do you anticipate continuing active membership? Why or why not?

II Membership Meaning

When you first joined, what was your original reason for membership?
How did your own racial/ethnic identity impact your decision to join a BGLO?
How has your purpose for membership changed throughout your time in your BGLO?
How has membership in a BGLO impacted you?

- In what ways has membership impacted your view of race and/or discrimination?

How has your membership impacted your BGLO?
Describe your university campus [probe for the following]:

- Racial composition of campus.
- Racial composition of BGLOs.
- Location [city, state and/or region] and school type [e.g., public, private, urban, suburban].

III Conceptions of Racial Identity

How would you describe your racial/ethnic identity?

- [if more than one] Is there one racial/ethnic group that you most identify with? Why/why not?
- How has the way you identify yourself changed over time, if at all?

How do others describe your racial/ethnic identity?

- Do you agree/disagree? Why?
- Why do others identify you in that way?

How does your racial/ethnic identity affect you? [probe for the following]:

- Friendships.
- Opportunities.
- Interests.
- Has this changed over time? In what ways and/or why?

Would you say that being ___ [race/ethnic identity] is important to you? Why/why not?

- Can you think of times in your life when it has been more/less important?

Now I'd like to ask you about any experiences you might have had with racism or discrimination when you were growing up [then within BGLO].

- What happened?
- How often?
- Where?
- Perpetrators?
- Who came to your aid? What did they do or say?
- Can you describe to me how these experiences made you feel?
- Did you share these experiences with anyone? How did they respond? If not your parents, why not? How about other family members?
- How have your experiences with or understanding of discrimination changed over time?

So tell me about your friends growing up:

- Race/ethnicity of closest friends.
- Did you seek out people of similar race/ethnicity? Why/why not?

When you were growing up, how conscious do you think you were of being ____ [race/ethnicity]?

- What prompted this consciousness?
- When did this consciousness begin?
- Feelings toward this consciousness?

[if respondent has not described hometown] Tell me about where you grew up [probe for the following]:

- Geographic location.
- Demographics.
- Family's friends and/or social networks.

How important do you think it was to your family that you be familiar with your racial/ethnic culture?

- What aspects?
- Who felt it was important and how did they express this to you?
- Who took responsibility to teach you?

Did your family ever speak to you about racism or discrimination that you might face?

- What did they say to you?
- Did they suggest any coping strategies for dealing with incidents?
- How comfortable did you feel in talking about racism with them?

IV Social Networks

Tell me about your closest friends in college.

- Where and/or how you met.
- Race/ethnicity.

Some people say that college is a time for exploring one's identity. How true was this for you?

- [if yes] What motivated your interest?
- What did you do to explore your identity?
- [if no] Why not?

Now I'd like to ask you some questions about your dating history.
What has been the racial/ethnic background of people you have dated in the past?

- Any racial/ethnic preferences?
- What about currently? Who do you find yourself attracted to?

Are you married now or currently in a relationship?

- What is the race/ethnicity of your partner [for those in interracial/ interethnic relationships]?
- How did/do your respective families respond to your relationship?
- Is anybody else in your families involved in an interracial/interethnic relationship?
- To what extent does race or ethnicity shape the life you have created with your partner?
- Do you have children or plan to have children?
- How important is it to you that your (future) children know about their ethnic roots?
- What will you do/have you done to accomplish this?
- Will you speak/have you spoken with your children about racism or discrimination that they might face?
- [if yes] What might/did you say?

Have you ever felt out of place or uncomfortable because of your race/ethnicity?

- What was the situation?

Has anybody ever made assumptions about you based on larger ethnic or racial stereotypes?

- What was the situation?

Do you believe there is racial discrimination in the United States today? [for interviews after Michael Brown shooting probe for the following]:

- Ferguson and/or Michael Brown.
- Eric Garner.
- BGLO activities around police brutality.

In terms of comfort, with which racial/ethnic groups are you:

- Most socially comfortable?
- Least comfortable?
- Most accepted?
- Least accepted?
- What makes them feel more/less comfortable?
- Why do you think you're more/less accepted?

V Final Questions

[If respondent has not provided the following]:

- In what year did you become a member of your BGLO?
- How many members were on your line?
- Were any of the other members non-Black?
- Can you give me an idea as to how many non-Black members have joined your particular chapter before you and after you crossed?

If you had to choose just one, would you think of yourself mainly as a member of your particular ethnic/racial group, your nationality [e.g., American], or as a member of your BGLO?

Interview Guide – Attitudes Towards Race Relations

The Symbolic Racism 2000 Scale

1. It's really a matter of some people not trying hard enough; if blacks would only try harder they could be just as well off as whites.

   <1> Strongly agree
   <2> Somewhat agree

<3> Somewhat disagree
<4> Strongly disagree

2. Irish, Italian, Jewish and many other minorities overcame prejudice and worked their way up. Blacks should do the same.

<1> Strongly agree
<2> Somewhat agree
<3> Somewhat disagree
<4> Strongly disagree

3. Some say that black leaders have been trying to push too fast. Others feel that they haven't pushed fast enough. What do you think?

<1> Trying to push very much too fast
<2> Going too slowly
<3> Moving at about the right speed

4. How much of the racial tension that exists in the United States today do you think blacks are responsible for creating?

<1> All of it
<2> Most
<3> Some
<4> Not much at all

5. How much discrimination against blacks do you feel there is in the United States today, limiting their chances to get ahead?

<1> A lot
<2> Some
<3> Just a little
<4> None at all

6. Generations of slavery and discrimination have created conditions that make it difficult for blacks to work their way out of the lower class.

<1> Strongly agree
<2> Somewhat agree
<3> Somewhat disagree
<4> Strongly disagree

7. Over the past few years, blacks have gotten less than they deserve.

<1> Strongly agree
<2> Somewhat agree
<3> Somewhat disagree
<4> Strongly disagree

Have you ever felt out of place or uncomfortable because of your race/ethnicity?

- What was the situation?

Has anybody ever made assumptions about you based on larger ethnic or racial stereotypes?

- What was the situation?

Do you believe there is racial discrimination in the United States today? [for interviews after Michael Brown shooting probe for the following]:

- Ferguson and/or Michael Brown.
- Eric Garner.
- BGLO activities around police brutality.

In terms of comfort, with which racial/ethnic groups are you:

- Most socially comfortable?
- Least comfortable?
- Most accepted?
- Least accepted?
- What makes them feel more/less comfortable?
- Why do you think you're more/less accepted?

V Final Questions

[If respondent has not provided the following]:

- In what year did you become a member of your BGLO?
- How many members were on your line?
- Were any of the other members non-Black?
- Can you give me an idea as to how many non-Black members have joined your particular chapter before you and after you crossed?

If you had to choose just one, would you think of yourself mainly as a member of your particular ethnic/racial group, your nationality [e.g., American], or as a member of your BGLO?

Interview Guide – Attitudes Towards Race Relations

The Symbolic Racism 2000 Scale

1. It's really a matter of some people not trying hard enough; if blacks would only try harder they could be just as well off as whites.

    <1> Strongly agree
    <2> Somewhat agree

<3> Somewhat disagree
<4> Strongly disagree

2. Irish, Italian, Jewish and many other minorities overcame prejudice and worked their way up. Blacks should do the same.

    <1> Strongly agree
    <2> Somewhat agree
    <3> Somewhat disagree
    <4> Strongly disagree

3. Some say that black leaders have been trying to push too fast. Others feel that they haven't pushed fast enough. What do you think?

    <1> Trying to push very much too fast
    <2> Going too slowly
    <3> Moving at about the right speed

4. How much of the racial tension that exists in the United States today do you think blacks are responsible for creating?

    <1> All of it
    <2> Most
    <3> Some
    <4> Not much at all

5. How much discrimination against blacks do you feel there is in the United States today, limiting their chances to get ahead?

    <1> A lot
    <2> Some
    <3> Just a little
    <4> None at all

6. Generations of slavery and discrimination have created conditions that make it difficult for blacks to work their way out of the lower class.

    <1> Strongly agree
    <2> Somewhat agree
    <3> Somewhat disagree
    <4> Strongly disagree

7. Over the past few years, blacks have gotten less than they deserve.

    <1> Strongly agree
    <2> Somewhat agree
    <3> Somewhat disagree
    <4> Strongly disagree

8.   Over the past few years, blacks have gotten more economically than they deserve.

<1> Strongly agree
<2> Somewhat agree
<3> Somewhat disagree
<4> Strongly disagree

For more on the symbolic racism scale, see:
    Henry, P.J. and David O. Sears. 2002. "The Symbolic Racism 2000 Scale." *Political Psychology* 23(2): 253–283.

GLOSSARY

Black Greek-letter organization	BGLO
Charter line/Charter member	Initial pledge class of a new nationally approved chapter
Cross/Crossing	Refers to being formally initiated into a BGLO
Divine Nine	Refers to the nine organizations represented under the National Pan-Hellenic Council
Graduate chapter	Post-collegiate chapter of BGLO members
Inter-Fraternity Council	IFC, the association of collegiate men's fraternities, predominately white
Line	Pledge class; BGLO members who were initiated into their organization's chapter together
Line sister/brother	Pledge class members
Neophyte	A new member of a BGLO
National Pan-Hellenic Council	NPHC, the coordinating body for the nine historically Black sororities and fraternities
National Panhellenic Conference	Association of national and international sororities, predominantly white
Pledge/Pledging	Initiation process into a Greek-letter organization
Pledges	People undergoing initiation into a Greek-letter organization
Probate/Probate show	New member presentation

Prophyte	BGLO member who has initiated members
Soror	Sorority sister in BGLO parlance
The yard/On the yard	College campus where BGLO chapter(s) are present; can also refer to centralized outdoor meeting space on campus where BGLO members congregate

INDEX

Taylor & Francis eBooks

Helping you to choose the right eBooks for your Library

Add Routledge titles to your library's digital collection today. Taylor and Francis ebooks contains over 50,000 titles in the Humanities, Social Sciences, Behavioural Sciences, Built Environment and Law.

Choose from a range of subject packages or create your own!

Benefits for you

» Free MARC records
» COUNTER-compliant usage statistics
» Flexible purchase and pricing options
» All titles DRM-free.

REQUEST YOUR FREE INSTITUTIONAL TRIAL TODAY

Free Trials Available
We offer free trials to qualifying academic, corporate and government customers.

Benefits for your user

» Off-site, anytime access via Athens or referring URL
» Print or copy pages or chapters
» Full content search
» Bookmark, highlight and annotate text
» Access to thousands of pages of quality research at the click of a button.

eCollections – Choose from over 30 subject eCollections, including:

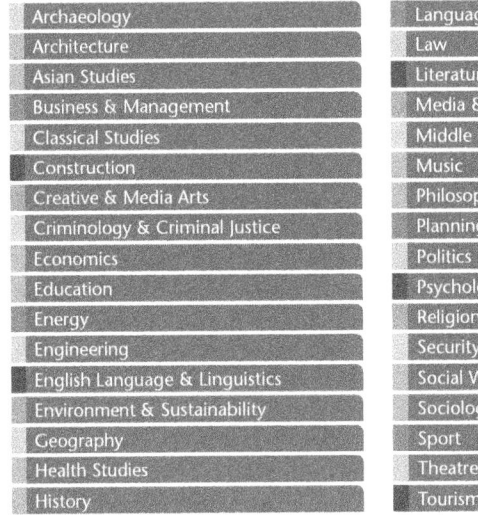

Archaeology	Language Learning
Architecture	Law
Asian Studies	Literature
Business & Management	Media & Communication
Classical Studies	Middle East Studies
Construction	Music
Creative & Media Arts	Philosophy
Criminology & Criminal Justice	Planning
Economics	Politics
Education	Psychology & Mental Health
Energy	Religion
Engineering	Security
English Language & Linguistics	Social Work
Environment & Sustainability	Sociology
Geography	Sport
Health Studies	Theatre & Performance
History	Tourism, Hospitality & Events

For more information, pricing enquiries or to order a free trial, please contact your local sales team:
www.tandfebooks.com/page/sales

 **Routledge**
Taylor & Francis Group

The home of
Routledge books

www.tandfebooks.com

2/15/19

CPSIA information can be obtained
at www.ICGtesting.com
Printed in the USA
LVHW011243300119
605791LV00004B/469

9 781138 629639